WITH EYES AND SOUL
Images of Cuba

Let's Talk About It

Please Return to:

MAINE HUMANITIES COUNCIL

HARRIET P. HENRY CENTER FOR THE BOOK
674 Brighton Avenue   Portland, Maine 04102-1012
207-773-5051   fax 207-773-2416   www.mainehumanities.org

the power & pleasure of ideas
MAINE HUMANITIES

WITH EYES AND SOUL
Images of Cuba

Poems by Nancy Morejón
Photographs by Milton Rogovin

Edited by Dennis Maloney
Translated by Pamela Carmell and David Frye

WHITE PINE PRESS • BUFFALO, NEW YORK

Copyright ©2004 by Nancy Morejon
Copyright ©2004 by Milton Rogovin
Translations copyright ©2004 by Pamela Carmell and David Frye

All rights reserved. This work, or portions thereof, may not be reproduced in any form without the written permission of the publisher.

Publication of this book has been made possible,
in part, by grants from
the National Endowment for the Arts
and with public funds from
the New York State Council on the Arts, a State Agency.

First Editon

Printed and bound in the United States of America.

ISBN 1-893996-25-5

Library of Congress Control Number: 2004109159

Published by
White Pine Press
P.O. Box 236
Buffalo, New York 14201
www.whitepine.org

WITH EYES AND SOUL
Images of Cuba

Table of Contents

Al lector / 10
To the Reader / 11
Preludio / 14
Prelude / 15
Persona / 18
Persona / 19
Un patio de La Habana / 22
A Patio in Havana / 23
Mirar adentro / 26
Looking Inside / 26
Negro / 28
Black Man / 29
Siempre decían / 30
They Always Used to Say / 30
Naturaleza muerta / 32
Still Life / 33
El hogar / 36
Home / 37
Nuevo salmo / 40
New Psalm / 41
Monólogo del pescador / 44
Fisherman's Monologue / 45
Hilandera / 46
Spinner / 47
Restos del Coral Island / 50
The Wreck of the Coral Island / 51
Y arderán las banderas / 54
And the Flags Will Burn / 54
Mujeres nuevas / 56
New Woman / 57
Nueva fábula de albañil / 60
The New Fable of the Bricklayer / 60
Haremos la vida / 64
We Will Make A Life / 64
Obrera del tabaco / 66
Tobacco Worker / 67

Antonia Eiriz / 70
Antonia Eiriz / 71
Alquimia / 72
Alchemy / 73
Los Artesanos / 76
The Artisans / 77
Cerco / 80
Siege / 81
Patria / 83
Homeland / 83
Elogio de la danza / 86
In Praise of Dance / 87
Elogio de las pequeñas bailarinas / 88
In Praise of These Young Dancers / 89
La cena / 90
Supper / 91
Pareja negra / 96
Black Couple / 97
Instante / 100
Instant / 101
Hora de la verdad (IX) / 104
Hour of Truth (IX) / 105
En Moa / 108
In Moa / 109

Nancy Morejón / 111
Milton Rogovin / 113
The Translators / 115

To the Reader / Al lector

Estos poemas se escribieron entre los veranos de 1986 y 1987. Algunos no son exactamente poemas aunque se lo hayan propuesto. Son prosas, viñetas —como quiera llamárseles— al servicio de la imagen fotográfica que el artista Milton Rogovin creó entre el ir y venir de los cubanos en su medio habitual. La mayoría de estos textos nació de un destello en donde, a veces, se anula la poetisa y predomina siempre el lector como un rey noble. Pero también nacieron del entusiasmo que me causaron las fotos de este mago de la realidad quien, un día, llevado de la mano por Naty Revuelta, apareció en La Habana para fusionarnos, los tres, en un proyecto que culminaría en un objeto de arte que cantara, con buenos ojos, a la vida cubana de hoy. Muy pronto nos dimos cuenta de que algunos de los personajes de Milton, así como ciertos contextos ya estaban presentes, de una forma u otra, en varios poemas míos. Por eso es que se incluyen poemas publicados en libros anteriores.

Escribir poesía con esta idea de trabajo aplicado, como quien borda un mantel para uso de sus seres queridos, levanta el ánimo y enriquece el conocimiento. Esta poesía es de oficio y beneficio, de esfuerzo y placer, de palabras al viento con signos de amor muy fijos en la tierra natal.

Agradezco a Milton Rogovin sus hermosísimas fotos y la oportunidad de trabajar con ellas.

Agradezco a Naty Revuelta su aliento, el regalo mismo de Milton Rogovin.

Y, sobre todo, le agradezco infinitamente a nuestra gente.

—Nancy Morejón
La Habana, 4 de agosto de 1987

These poems were written between the summers of 1986 and 1987. Some of them are not quite the poems they were intended to be. They are prose poems, vignettes, whatever you prefer to call them, placed at the service of the photographic images that the artist Milton Rogovin has created from the comings and goings of Cubans in their everyday milieu. Most of these texts were born from that flash of light in which the poetess sometimes loses her identity, and where the reader always reigns as a noble king. But they were also born from the enthusiasm that I caught from the photographs of that magician of reality who appeared one day, led by the hand of Naty Revuelta, in Havana, where the three of us joined in a project to create an object of art, a hymn to be sung, with eyes and soul, to life in Cuba today. We quickly realized that some of Milton's characters and some of his contexts were already present in one form or another in several of my poems. That is why some previously published poems have been included.

Writing poetry with this idea of applied work, like someone who embroiders a tablecloth to be used by her loved ones, raises one's spirits and enriches one's understanding. This is a poetry of effort and pleasure, of function and favor, of words thrown to the winds with signs of love firmly fixed in their native soil.

I thank Milton Rogovin for his beautiful photographs and for the opportunity to work with them.

I thank Naty Revuelta for her strength of spirit, the same gift Milton Rogovin gives.

And above all, I give endless thanks to our people.

—Nancy Morejón
Havana, August 4, 1987

(D.F.)

WITH EYES AND SOUL
Images of Cuba

In Memory of Anne Rogovin

Preludio

Mi patria es dulce por fuera, y muy amarga por dentro, escribió Nicolás Guillén, en la Argentina, hacia finales de los años cuarenta. Nuestra historia transcurría así, en medio de cañaverales amargos y ajenos, junto a inmensas vegas de tabaco olorosas y ajenas, entre corales y arrecifes ajenos, bajo un aire que respirábamos ajeno. Cuba era "un palmar vendido". Y lo único que poseíamos a plenitud era el hambre en la madrugada, en el cenit del día, a la intemperie; el látigo y la pena bronca, la descomunal ignorancia del mundo y de nosotros mismos; unos dioses oscuros sin horizonte apenas y un montón de esperanzas que un día, desde la alta Sierra, asaltaron la Isla, en pleno corazón del Caribe. La Habana ardía como los ojos de un gallo. La penumbra iba huyendo por encima de los cocoteros. Un viento verde se instaló en la mañana.

Prelude

My country is sweet on the outside, but very bitter on the inside, wrote Nicolás Guillén, in Argentina, at the end of the 1940s. That's how our history happened: in the midst of cane fields that were bitter and belonged to others, along endless plantations of tobacco that were fragrant and belonged to others, among coral shoals and reefs that belonged to others, under the air we breathed that belonged to others. Cuba was a *palm grove that was sold*. And the only thing we fully owned was hunger at early rising, at the height of day, in wind and weather; the lash and rude pain; the boundless ignorance of the world and of ourselves; a few dim gods with no horizon; and loads of hopes, which one day, from the heights of the Sierra, assaulted the Island in the very heart of the Caribbean. Havana burned like the eyes of a cock. Night's shadows fled above the coconut palms. A green wind settled in the morning.

(D.F.)

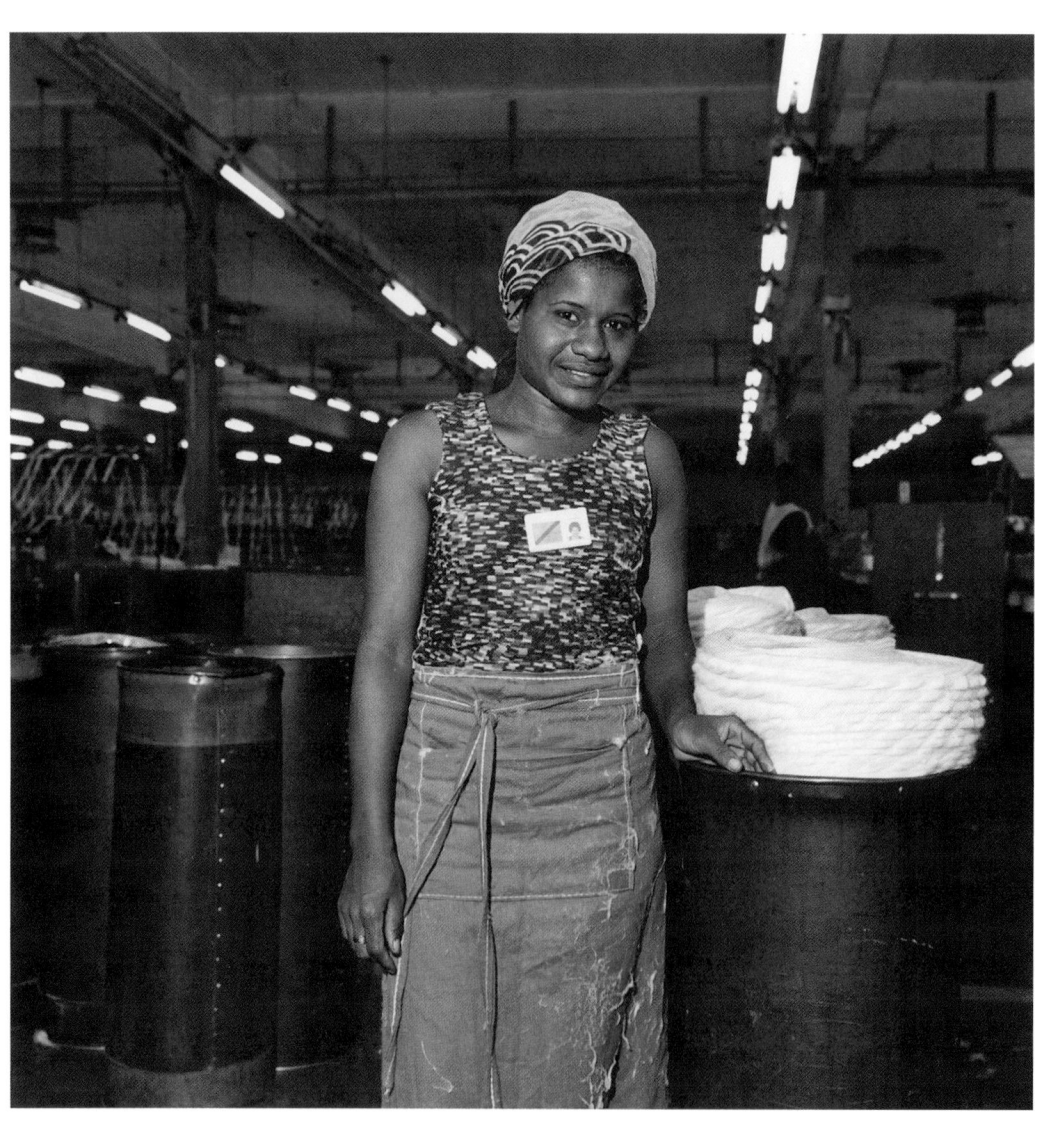

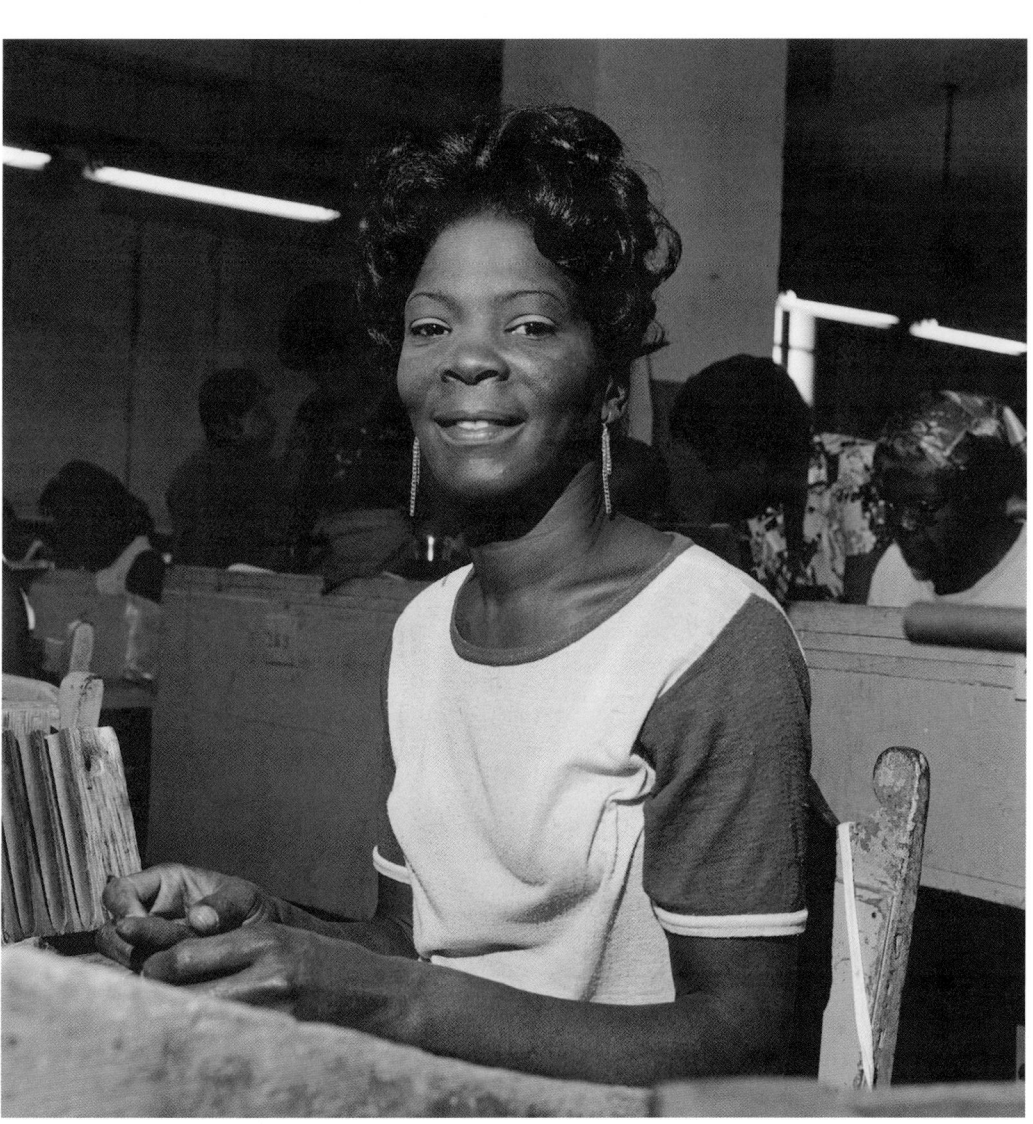

Persona

¿Cuál de estas mujeres soy yo?
¿O no soy yo la que está hablando
tras los barrotes de una ventana sin estilo
que da a la plenitud de todos estos siglos?
¿Acaso seré yo la mujer negra y alta
que corre y casi vuela
y alcanza *records* astronómicos,
con sus oscuras piernas celestiales
en su espiral de lunas?
¿En cuál músculo suyo se dibuja mi rostro,
clavado allí como un endecasílabo importado
de un país de nieve prohibida?

Estoy en la ventana
y cruza "la mujer de Antonio";
"la vecinita de enfrente", de una calle sin formas;
"la madre—negra Paula Valdés—".
¿Quién es el señorito que sufraga
sus ropas y sus viandas
y los olores de vetiver ya desprendidos de su andar?
¿Qué permanece en mí de esa mujer?
¿Qué nos une a las dos? ¿Qué nos separa?
¿O seré yo la "vagabunda del alba",
que alquila taxis en la noche de los jaguares
como una garza tendida en el pavimento
después de haber sido cazada
     y esquilmada
     y revendida
por la Quinta de los Molinos
y los embarcaderos del puerto?
Ellas: ¿quiénes serán? ¿o soy yo misma?
¿Quiénes son éstas que se parecen tanto a mí
no sólo por los colores de sus cuerpos
sino por ese humo devastador
que exhala nuestra piel de res marcada
por un extraño fuego que no cesa?

Persona

Which of these women is me?
Or am I not the one who's talking
behind the thick bars of a nondescript window
that looks out on the abundance of all these eras?
Might I be the tall, black woman
who runs, who nearly flies,
who sets astronomical records,
with her dark celestial legs
spiralling like moons?
Which of her muscles reflects my face,
fixed there like an imported line of poetry
from a land where snow is forbidden?

I'm at the window
and there goes "*la mujer de Antonio,*"
"*la vecinita de enfrente,*" crossing a shapeless street;
"*la madre—negra Paula Valdés—.*"
Which is the young Andalusian *don* who antes up for
her clothes and her vittles
and the smell of vetiver root she scatters as she walks?
What's left in me of this woman?
What holds the two of us together? What separates us?
Or might I be the "early morning wanderer"
who takes taxis in the night of jaguars
like a heron fallen to the pavement
after being hunted
and wasted
and resold
around the Quinta de los Molinos
and the piers of the port?
Who are they, these women? Or are they me?
Who are they, who look so much like me
not only in the color of their bodies
but in the devastating smoke
that rises from our animal hides, branded
by a strange, unceasing fire?

¿Por qué soy yo? ¿Por qué son ellas?

¿Quién es esa mujer
que está en todas nosotras huyendo de nosotras,
huyendo de su enigma y de su largo origen
con una incrédula plegaria entre los labios
o con un himno cantado
después de una batalla siempre renacida?

Todos mis huesos, ¿serán míos?
¿de quién serán todos mis huesos?
¿Me los habrán comprado
en aquella plaza remota de Gorée?
¿Toda mi piel será la mía
o me han devuelto a cambio
los huesos y la piel de otra mujer
cuyo vientre ha marcado otro horizonte,
otro ser, otras criaturas, otro dios?

Estoy en la ventana.
Yo sé que hay alguien.
Yo sé que una mujer ostenta mis huesos y mi carne;
que me ha buscado en su gastado seno
y que me encuentra en la vicisitud y el extravío.
La noche está enterrada en nuestra piel.
La sabia noche recompone sus huesos y los míos.
Un pájaro del cielo ha trocado su luz en nuestros ojos.

Why am I me? Why are they them?

Who is that woman,
the one in us all fleeing from us all,
fleeing her enigma and her long origin
with an incredulous prayer on her lips,
or singing a hymn
after a battle always being refought?

My bones: are they all mine?
Whose are all these bones?
Did they buy them for me
in that far-off plaza in Gorée?
Is all my skin my own,
or did they trade it to me
for the skin and bones of another woman
whose womb once marked another horizon,
another self, other beings, another god?

I'm at the window.
I know someone's there.
I know there's a woman flaunting my bones and my flesh;
know she's looked for me in her worn-out breast
and has found me, miserable and straying.
Night is rooted in our skin.
Wise night rebuilds her bones and mine.
A bird from the sky has transposed its light into our eyes.

(D.F.)

Un patio de la Habana

A Gerardo Fulleda León

Un patio de La Habana,
como pedía Machado,
es caro a la memoria.
Sin altos muros,
sin esa lumbre intrépida
del arcoiris,
sin la flor andaluza
que tanto abuela reclamaba
en los búcaros...

Un patio de La Habana
conserva huesos de los muertos
porque ellos son anchos tesoros,
viejas semillas de labrador.

Un patio, ay, de donde sale
tanta estrella.

A Patio in Havana

For Gerardo Fulleda León

A patio in Havana,
the kind Machado invoked,
is something memory holds dear.
With no high walls,
nor the intrepid splendor
of a rainbow,
nor the Andalusian flower
grandmother so stubbornly raised
in flowerpots...

A patio in Havana
preserves the bones of the dead
because they are vast treasures,
a farmer's age-old seeds.

A patio, ay, from which arise
so many stars.

(P.C.)

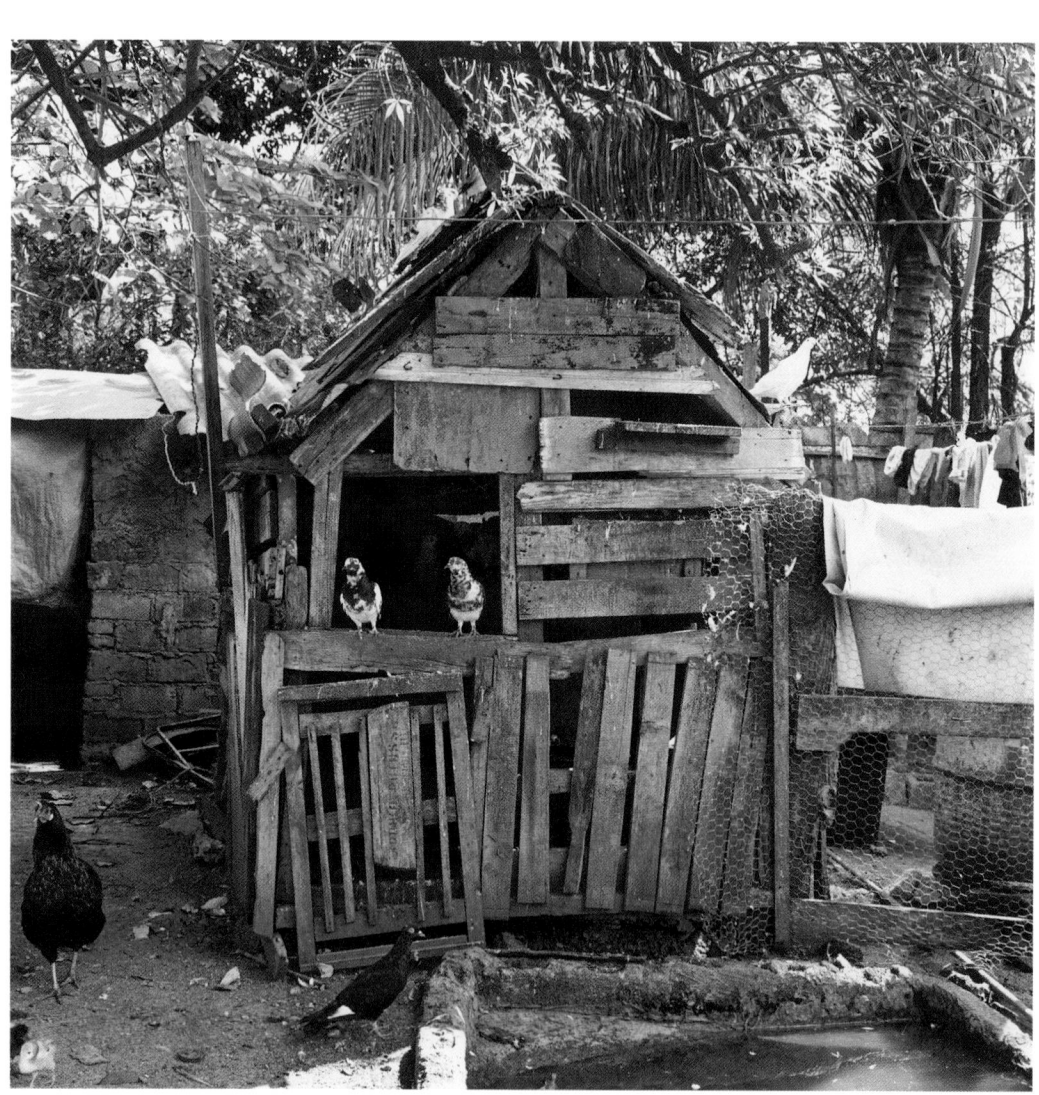

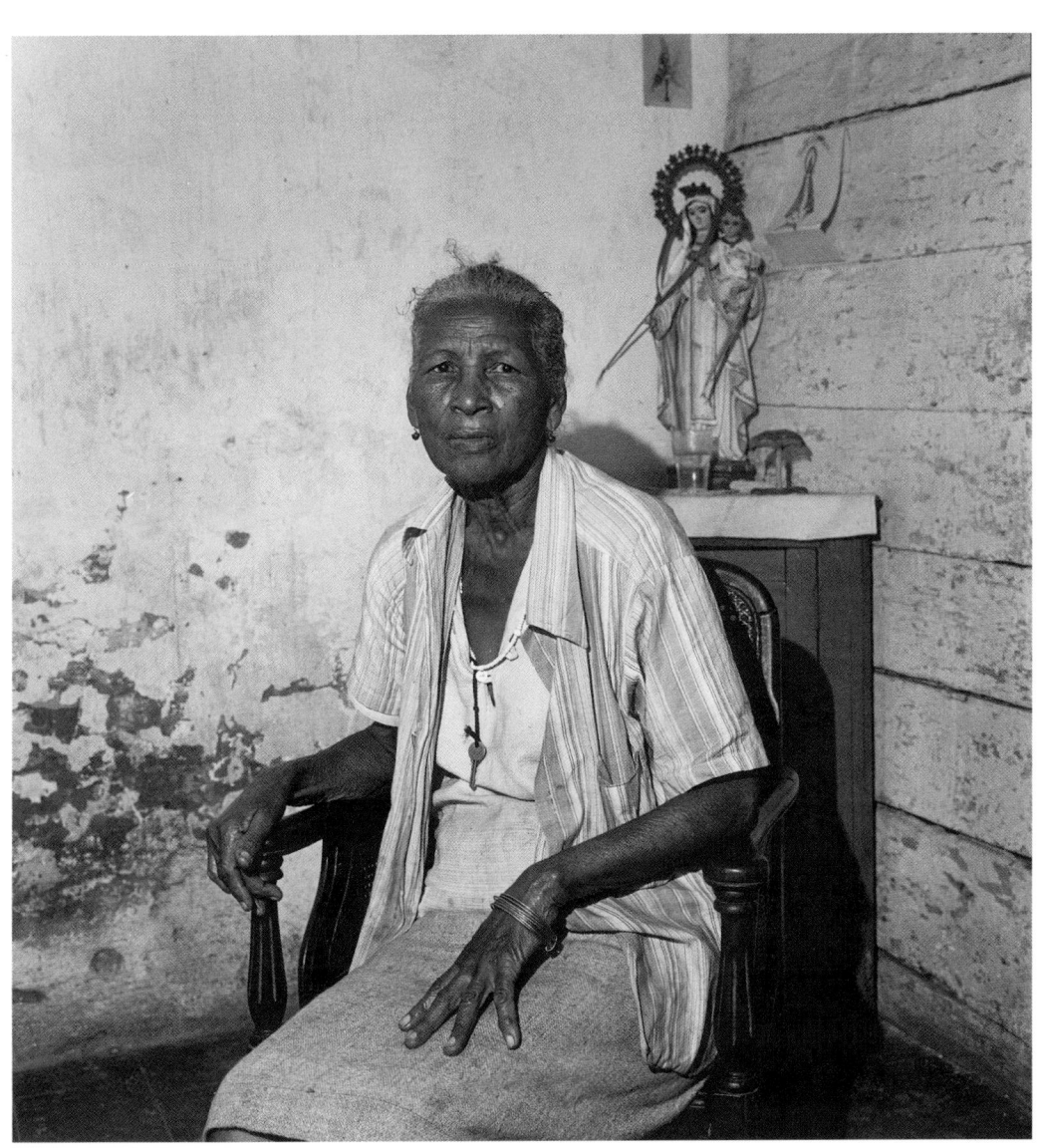

Mirar adentro

Del siglo XVI data mi pena
y apenas lo sabía
porque aquel ruiseñor
siempre canta en mi pena.

Looking Inside

My grief dates from the sixteenth century
and I scarcely knew it
because that nightingale
always sings in my grief.

(D.F.)

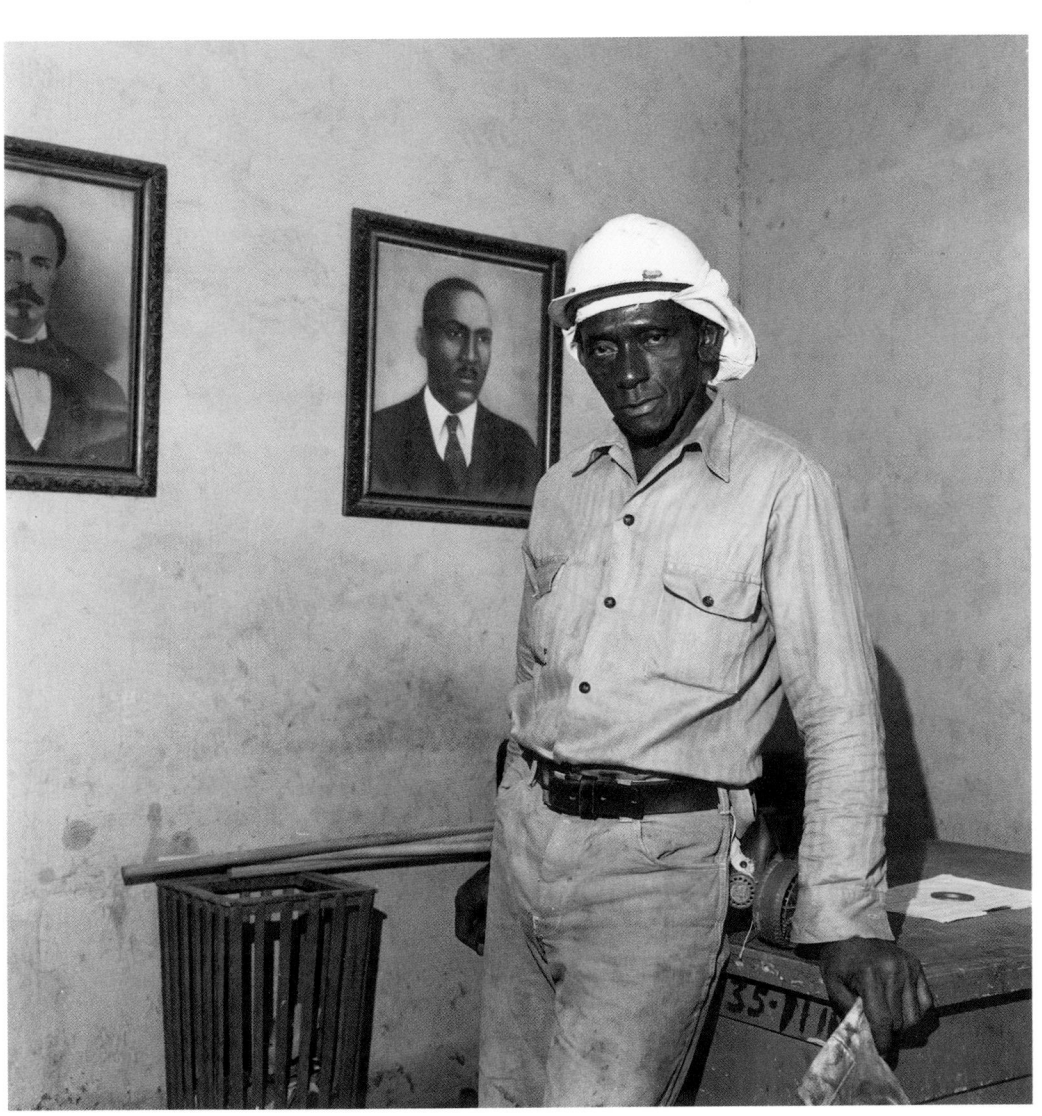

Negro

Tu pelo,
       para algunos,
era diablura del infierno;
pero el zunzún allí
puso su nido, sin reparos,
cuando pendías en lo alto del horcón,
frente al palacio
            de los capitanes.
Dijeron, sí, que el polvo del camino
te hizo infiel y violáceo,
como esas flores invernales
del trópico, siempre
tan asombrosas y arrogantes.
            Ya moribundo
sospechan que tu sonrisa era salobre
y tu musgo impalpable para el encuentro del amor.
Otros afirman que tus palos de monte
nos trajeron ese daño sombrío
que no nos deja relucir ante Europa
y que nos lanza, en la vorágine ritual,
a ese ritmo imposible
de los tambores innombrables.
Nosotros amaremos por siempre
tus huellas y tu ánimo de bronce
porque has traído esa luz viva del pasado fluyente,
ese dolor de haber entrado limpio a la batalla,
ese afecto sencillo por las campanas y los ríos,
ese rumor de aliento libre en primavera
que corre al mar para volver
                y volver a partir.

Black Man

Your hair,
         some said,
was the devil's work from hell;
but the hummingbird built
her nest there, never hesitating,
as you dangled on high from the beam,
in front of the palace
         of the captains.
They said, yes, dust from the road
made you disloyal and blue-black,
like those winter flowers
from the tropics, always
so astonishing and haughty.
                    Now as you are dying
they suspect that your smile was salty
and your moss too soft for the act of love.
Others assert that your sticks and branches
brought us this shadowy damage
which keeps us from shining in the eyes of Europe
and thrusts us into the ritual whirlpool,
into that impossible rhythm
of unnamable drums.
We will love forever
the mark you've left on us and your bronze spirit
because you brought that vibrant light from the past flowing by,
that pain of having entered the battle pure of heart,†
that honest fondness for bells and rivers,
that whisper of breath set free in the spring,
that races to the sea, comes back,
         then sets off again.

(P.C.)

Siempre decían

Siempre decían: "Unos lo llaman Lázaro. Otros lo llaman Babalú Ayé". Todavía hoy, no se sabe por cuál firme misterio, unos y otros acuden al Rincón—un pueblecito extraño y recoleto cuya maravilla deslumbra a cualquier viajero— en oleadas silvestres, para clamar o darle gracias mientras colocan bajo sus pies leprosos sacos de harina inmensos y vacíos, escobas relucientes, flores moradas como nísperos, cuentas de todos los colores y muletas sin dueño. Siempre oirás que te dicen: "Unos lo llaman Lázaro. Otros lo llaman Babalú Ayé".

They Always Used to Say

They always used to say: "Some call him Lazarus. Others call him Babalú Ayé." Even today, for who knows what unflinching reason, both groups journey to El Rincón—a strange and quiet little town whose marvelous secret dazzles every visitor—in surging waves, to cry out loud or give him thanks, while placing at his leprous feet immense and empty flour sacks, sparkling brooms, flowers that are the purple of sapodillas, beads of every color, and crutches unneeded by their owners. You will always hear them tell you: "Some call him Lazarus. Others call him Babalú Ayé."

(D.F.)

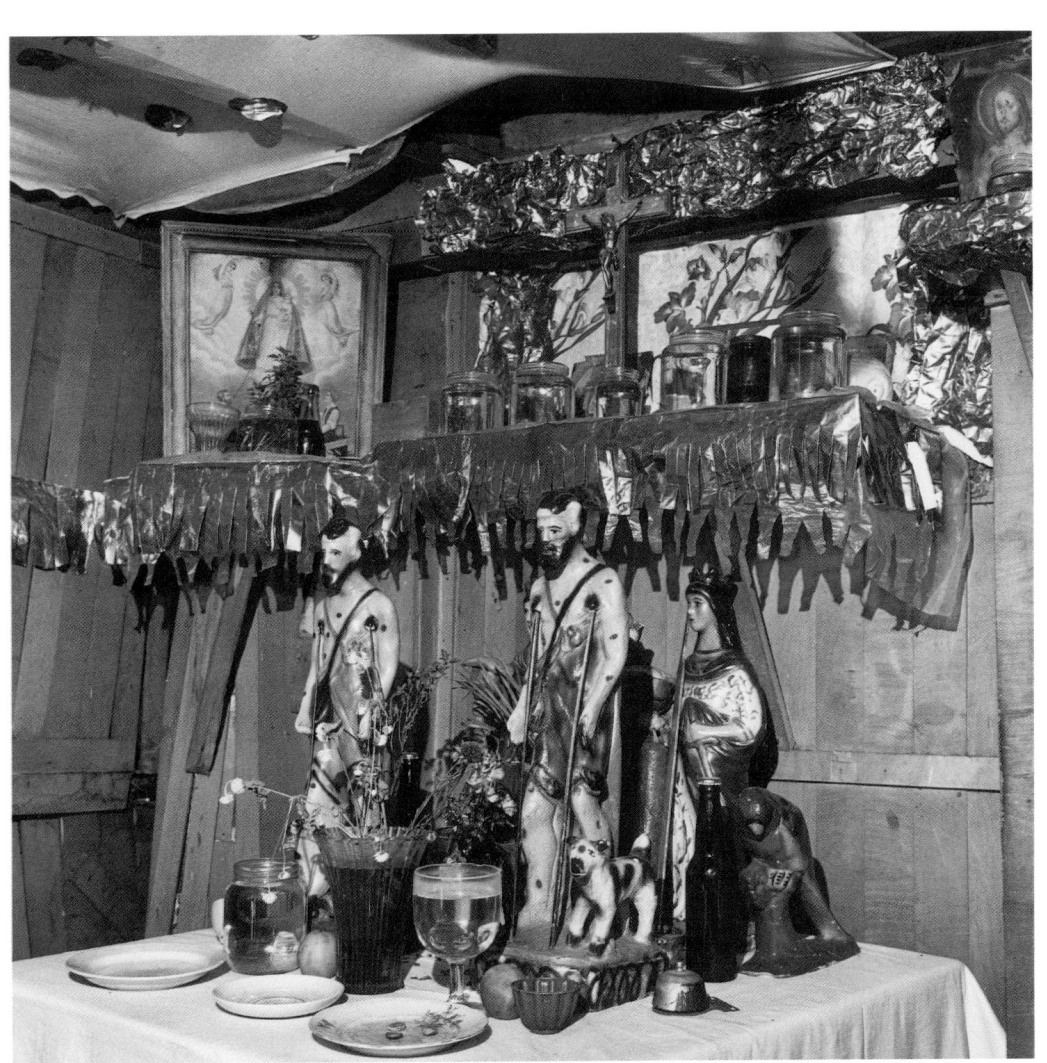

Naturaleza muerta

Me gusta contemplar las cosas
en su luz, sin que la mano del pintor
(¡Pobre Rembrandt!) toque ninguna
de sus transparencias.
Me gusta contemplar las cosas
en el trópico.
¿Cuál será la real belleza de las cosas?
¿Dónde estará la real belleza de las cosas?
Una mazorca viva y el humo que se incrusta
en las maderas polvorientas
con su mar de botellas sin fin
y las cazuelas hirvientes del verano.
Mirar los zumos de los jarros
como un jardín colgante
de Babilonia
al que me asomo todas las mañanas.
Ver los olores exactos de las tapas
que convocan al niño y a la anciana.
Y los techos mojados,
y los restos de coco,
los bancos del pasado, las láminas desdibujadas
y, sobre todo, la telaraña de siemprevivas
alzándose hacia el cielo
hasta fomar un arcoiris.

Still Life

I like to observe things
in their own light, the hand of the painter
(Poor Rembrandt!) not touching any part
of their transparent nature.
I like to observe things
in the tropics.
What could be the true beauty of things?
Where could the true beauty of those things lie?
A bright ear of corn and the smoke encrusted
in the dusty planks of wood
with their endless sea of bottles
and the boiling stewpot in the summer.
To peer at the juice kept in jars
like a Hanging Garden
of Babylon,
the garden that takes me by surprise every morning.
To see the distinct smells from the lids
that beckon the child and the old woman.
And the damp roofs,
and the coconut shells,
the benches from another era, the blurry prints
and, above all, the spider web of immortelle flowers
stretching wildly toward the sky
till it forms a rainbow.

(P.C.)

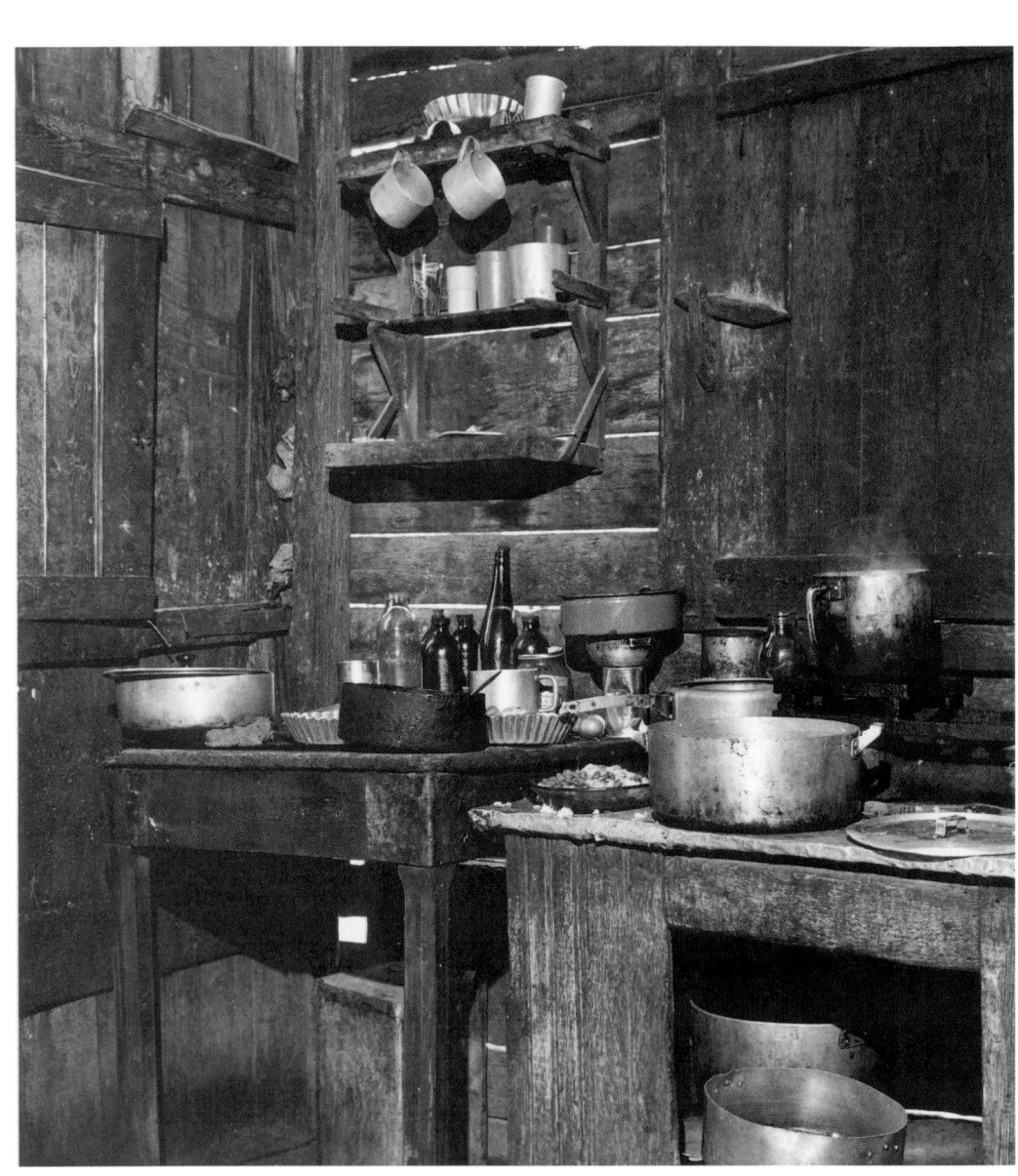

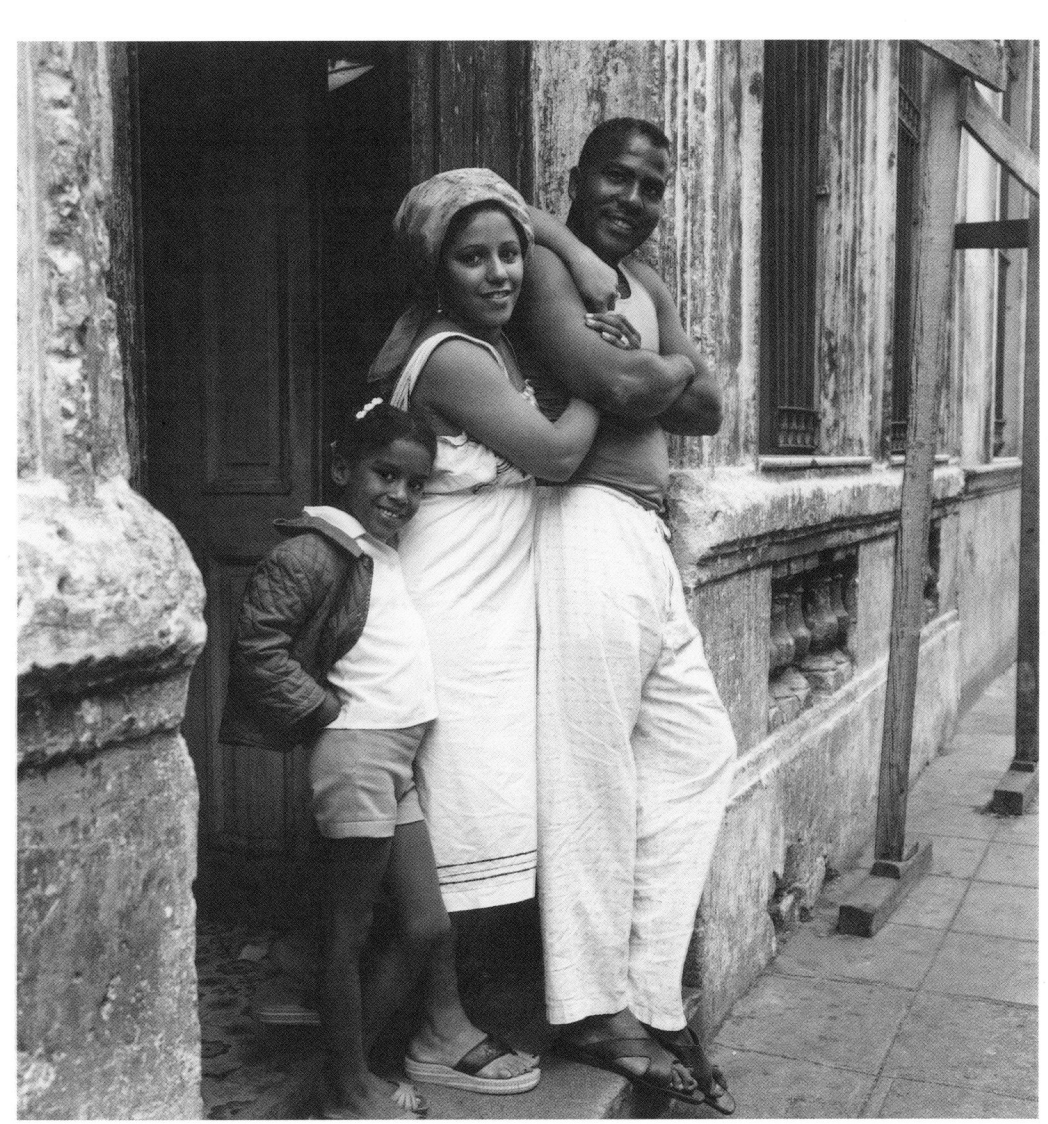

El hogar

Así es el hogar.

¿Suave brisa o manchas de alquitrán?
¿Pinchos de hielo o cálida magnesia?
¿Estertor o desidia?

Es un claro domingo del hogar,
donde ni la mañana, ni la tarde,
ni la noche y su ocaso se hacen indefinibles.
Es un domingo hijo de la naturaleza del hogar.
Ácido como un cítrico, es
un hogar de trabajos y lágrimas. Es
el domingo que se provee de tíos nostálgicos,
ahijados, pensamientos,
primos sin dimensión,
ayes, maledicencias.

El hogar sin recursos, de telaraña,
el hogar poco: el amargo,
el escaso, el sufrido, el penado,
el sin juguetes toscos o lujosos,
el sin lumbre para encender el fogón de carbones.
Es tan sólo un hogar para ahogar.
Un hogar que es el templo de un sano estibador:
Felipe o Fleitas o Candelario o Juan
—el suyo es un hogar muy hogar
de donde fueron desterrados los misales, las prédicas,
las promesas del paraíso celestial,
para poner en su lugar,
anémonas,
pargos
y carnadas.

Home

Home is like this.

A soft breeze or tar stains?
Icicles or warm milk of magnesia?
A death rattle or laziness?

It's a bright Sunday at home,
where neither morning, nor afternoon,
nor night and its setting sun are beyond definition.
It's a Sunday born of this home's nature.
Sour as a lemon, it's
a home of work and tears. It's
a Sunday furnished with nostalgic uncles,
godchildren, daydreams,
cousins beyond measure,
sighs, damnations.

A home with no resources, with spider webs,
a meager home: a bitter,
scarce, suffering, mourning
home with no toys, rough or luxurious,
a home without a flame to light its charcoal hearth.
It's a home in which to drown alone.
A home that is temple to a healthy stevedore:
Felipe or Fleitas or Candelario or Juan
—his is a very homey home
from which missals and sermons and promises of heaven
have been sent into exile,
to be replaced by
anemones,
porgies,
and bait.

(D.F.)

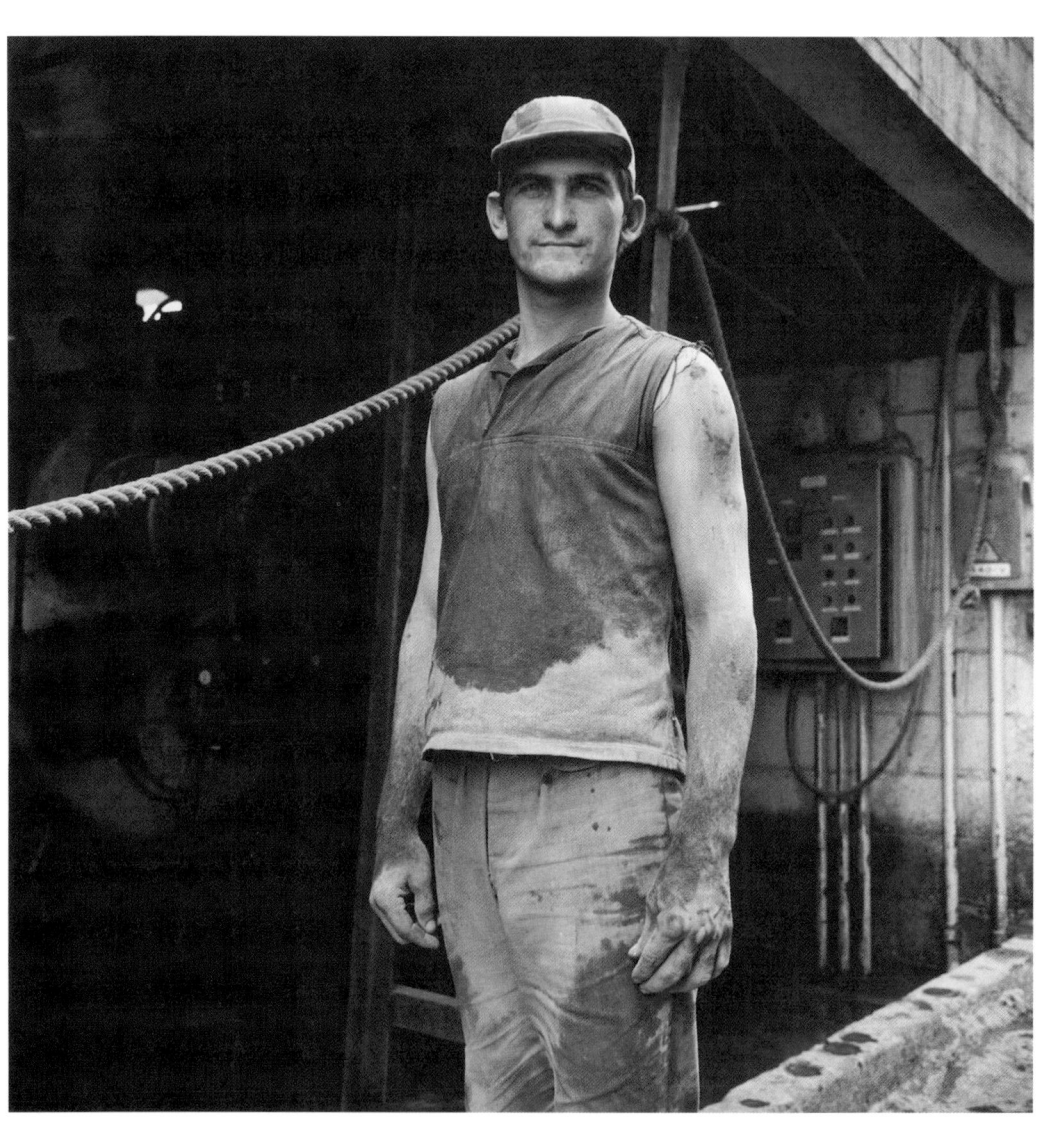

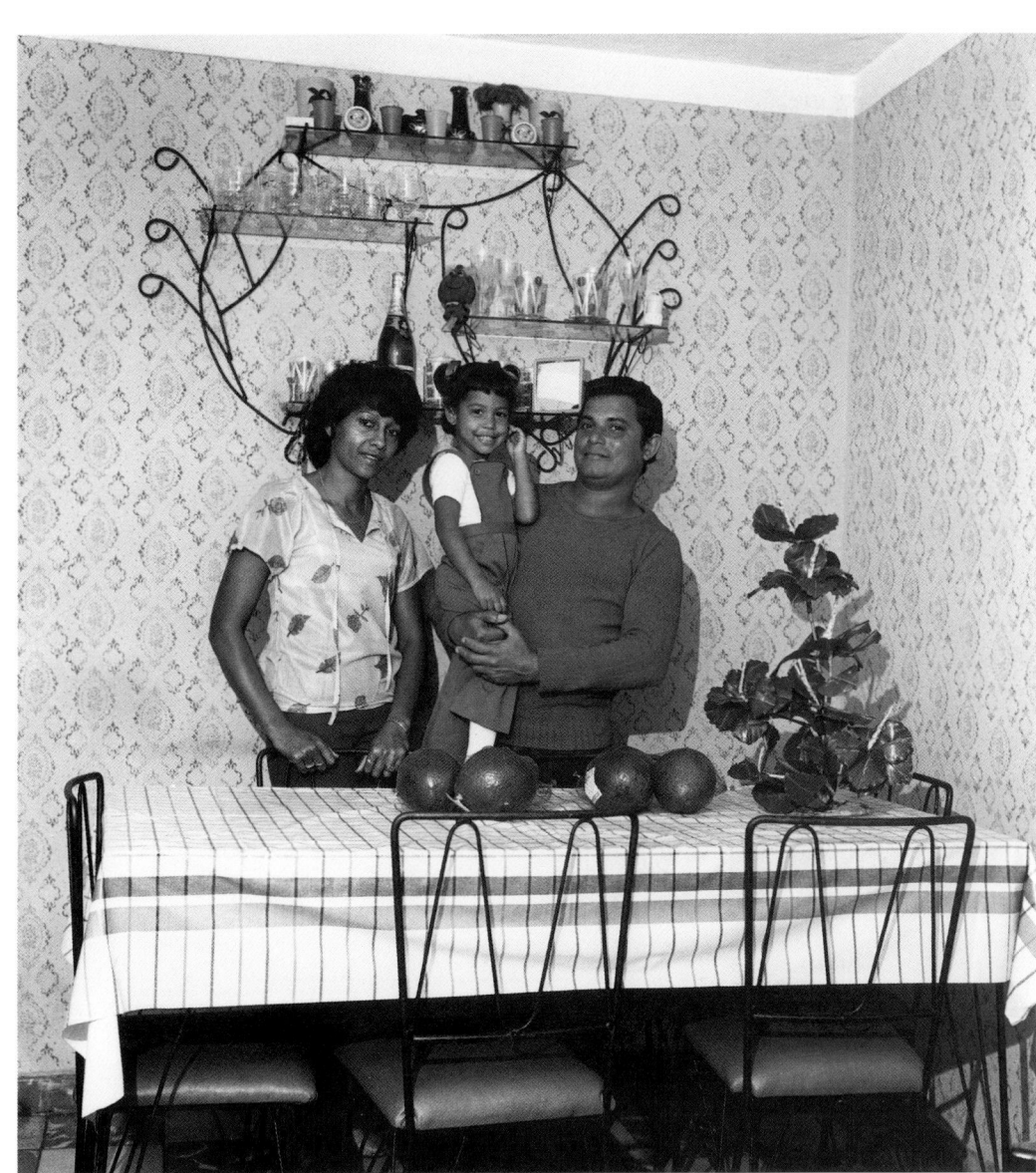

Nuevo salmo

Tú que aspiras a alcanzar
el don de las arenas
tú que sueles ignorar
el don de las arenas
ven hasta el borde del agua
y cálmala
tú que has guardado en tu ser
el don de las arenas

New Psalm

You who aspire to attain
the gift the sands have
you who always overlook
the gift the sands have
come right up to the water's edge
and calm the waves
you who have always had at your core
the gift the sands have

(P.C.)

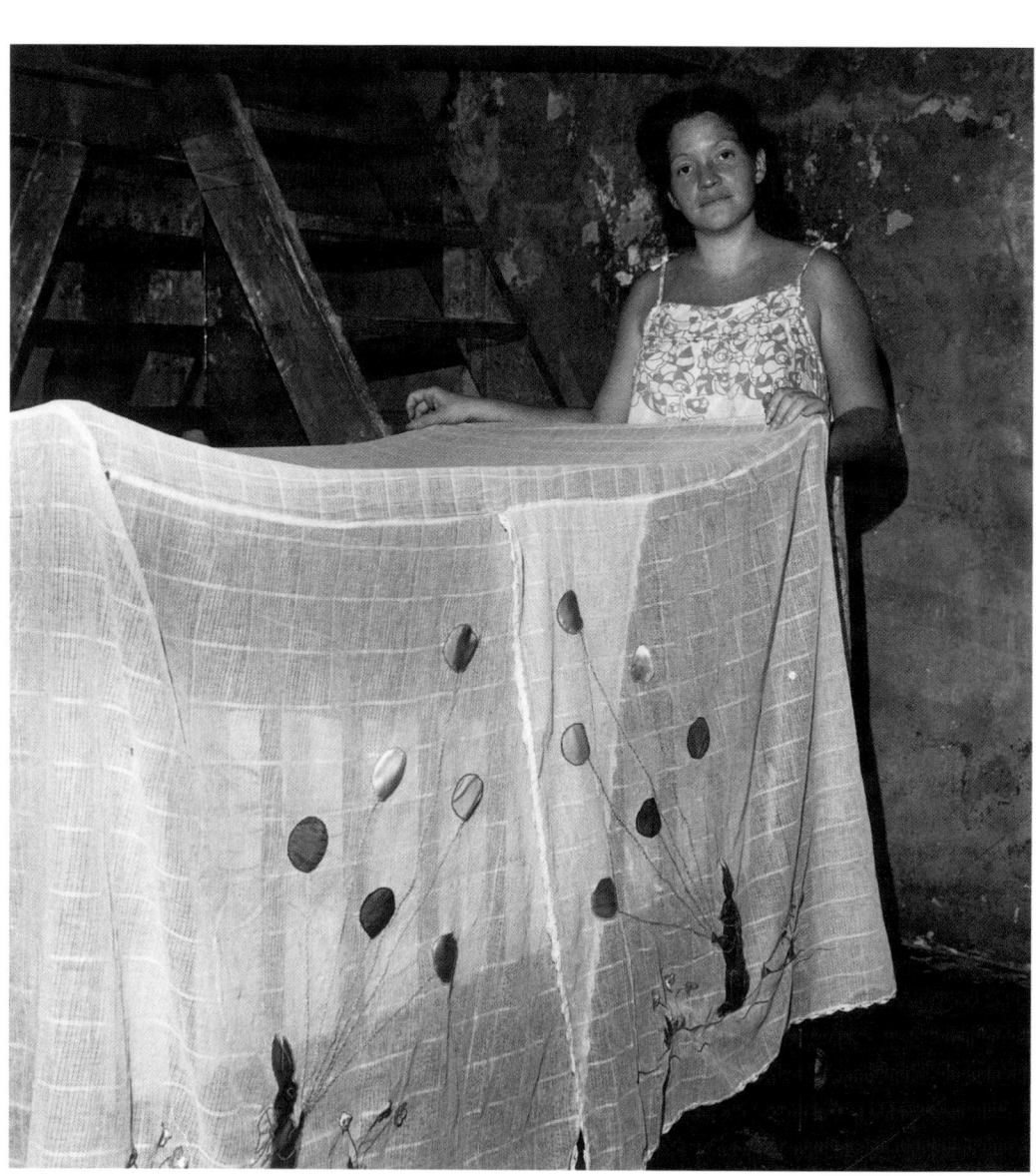

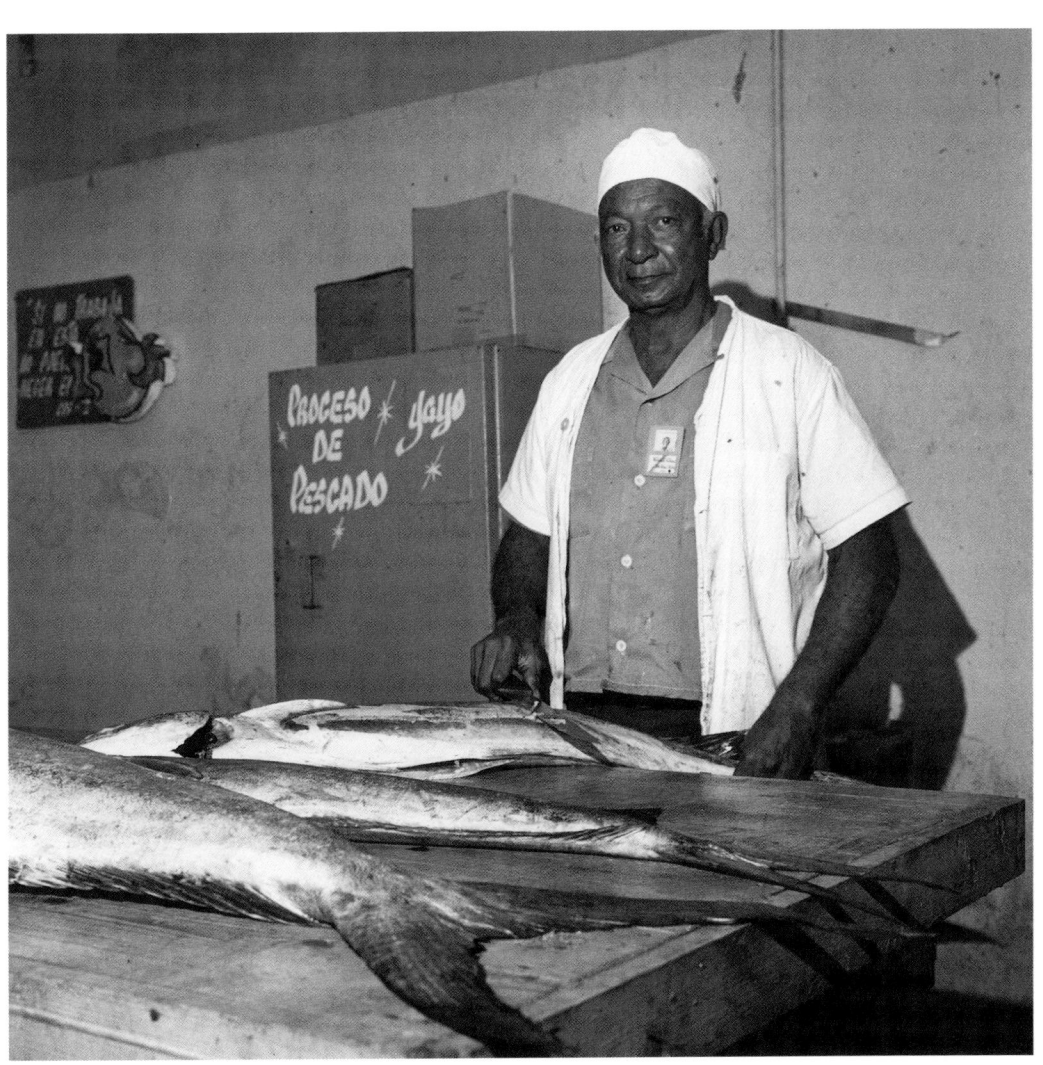

Monólogo del pescador

De niño, yo siempre soñaba con peces.
Que venía un chicherekú y me los arrancaba de la mano
después que tanto trabajo me había costado llegar al
fondo mismo del río, llenito de piedras, allá en la
desembocadura que iba a parar a la mar. Todo el mundo
decía "pez de agua dulce se va entre las manos". El pez de agua dulce se
escurre como el conejo en el monte y deja una línea
fosforescente que nunca se te olvida. Cómo quise coger
biajaibas y nunca lo conseguí. No me importaba si eran
de mar, si eran de río. Yo quería pescar peces, sacarlos
del agua con mis propias manos, mientras iba nadando.
Y en el camino, de la orilla a mi casa, hablarles de mil
cosas, que me contaran ellos las travesuras de los
chicherekús. Cosas de muchacho. Y ya ustedes ven, al
final, creo que mi sueño se ha cumplido.

Fisherman's Monologue

As a boy, I always dreamed about fish.
About how a *chichereku* goblin, the one in the old stories, would come
and snatch them out of my hand after I'd worked so hard
to get all the way to the bottom of the river, completely covered
with rocks, there at the mouth of the river that opened
to the sea. Everyone said, "Freshwater fish slip out of your hands."
Freshwater fish dart away like rabbits in the brush and leave a
phosphorescent trail you never forget. How I tried to catch
red-tailed *biajaiba* fish but never managed it. I didn't care if they
were from the ocean, if they were from the river. I wanted to catch
fish, pull them out of the water with my own hands as I swam along.
And on the road from the shore to my home, talk to them about a
thousand things, get them to tell me about the pranks the *chicherekus*
pull. Just a boy's foolish ideas. And now as you can all see, in the end,
I think my dream has come true.

(P.C.)

Hilandera

¿Quién no ha leído, alguna vez,
sobre las hilanderas?
En los cuentos de hadas
aparecen las bellas hilanderas
tocando nubes ciertas
con sus hilos inacabables,
empujando las sedas hacia el espacio
donde escuchamos una música
que brota desde sus conos blancos.
Los ojos avispados de esta hilandera
tienen la magia de los panes.
Su humanidad, sobre los puntos,
nos trajo eternamente
el viento huracanado de Lyon,
los perfumes de Persia.
Quiero que todos
volvamos a leer
sobre la historia
de las hilanderas.
Llévanos, hilandera, otra vez,
a los castillos verdes,
a aquellos puentes levadizos,
a las quimeras que tú fabricas hoy,
en medio de telares mecánicos
que te hacen más poderosa,
más tierna, más terrena.
Llévanos,
con tus manos,
hacia los sueños de la infancia.
Llévanos, hilandera, y danos tu alegría.

Spinner

Who hasn't read, once upon a time,
about women at their spinning wheels?
Beautiful spinners show up
in fairy tales
touching a group of clouds
with their unending threads,
casting silk threads into space
where we hear a kind of music
springing from their white cones.
The darting eyes of this spinner
have the magic of blessed bread.
Upon her bobbins, her human touch
has eternally brought us
hurricane winds from Lyon,
perfumes from Persia.
I want us all
to read again
the spinners' tale.
Spinner, lead us again
to green castles,
to drawbridges,
to the chimeras you construct today,
surrounded by mechanical looms
that make you more powerful,
more merciful, more earthly.
Lead us
with your hands,
back to the dreams of childhood.
Lead us back, spinner, and give us your joy.

(P.C.)

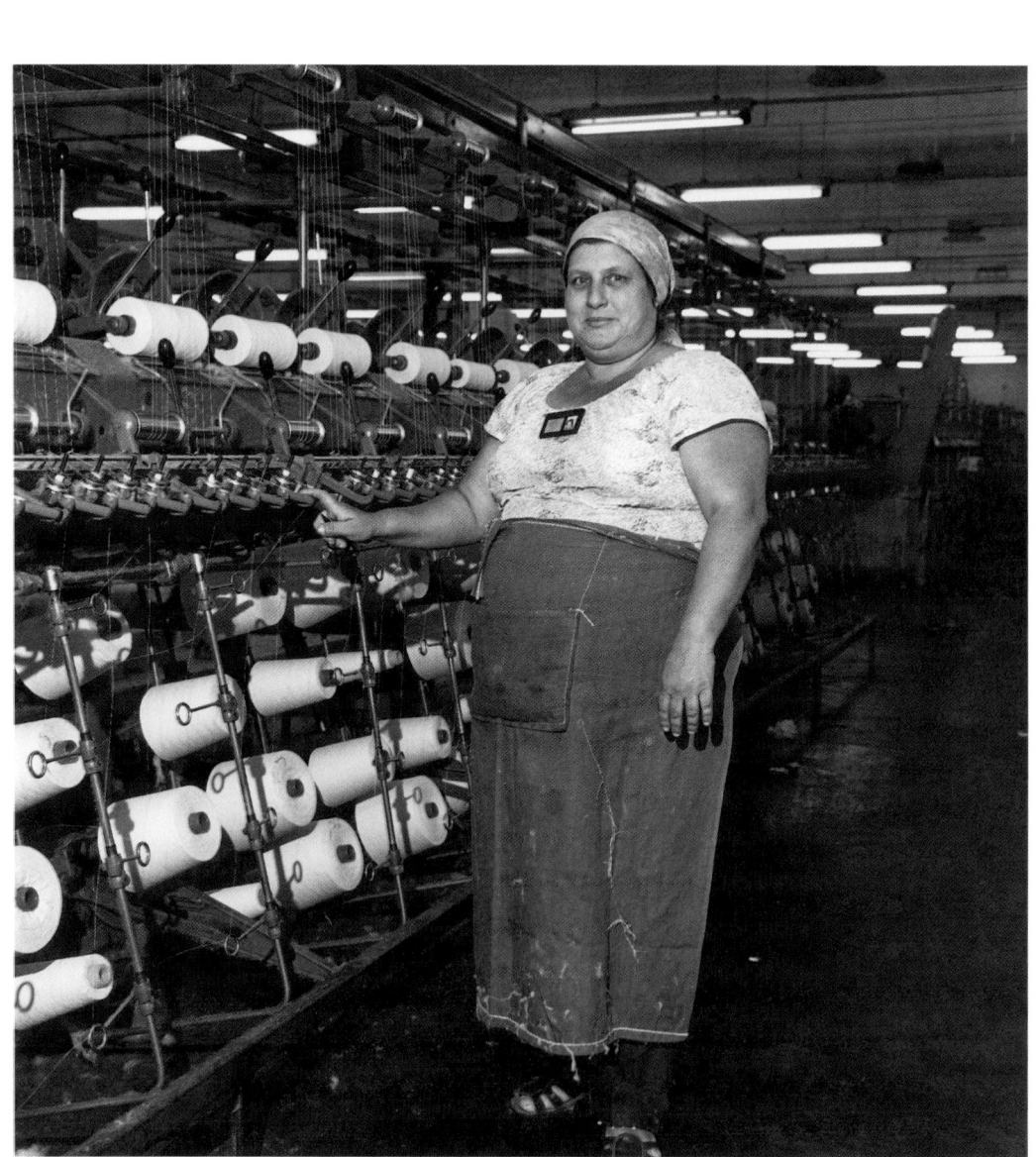

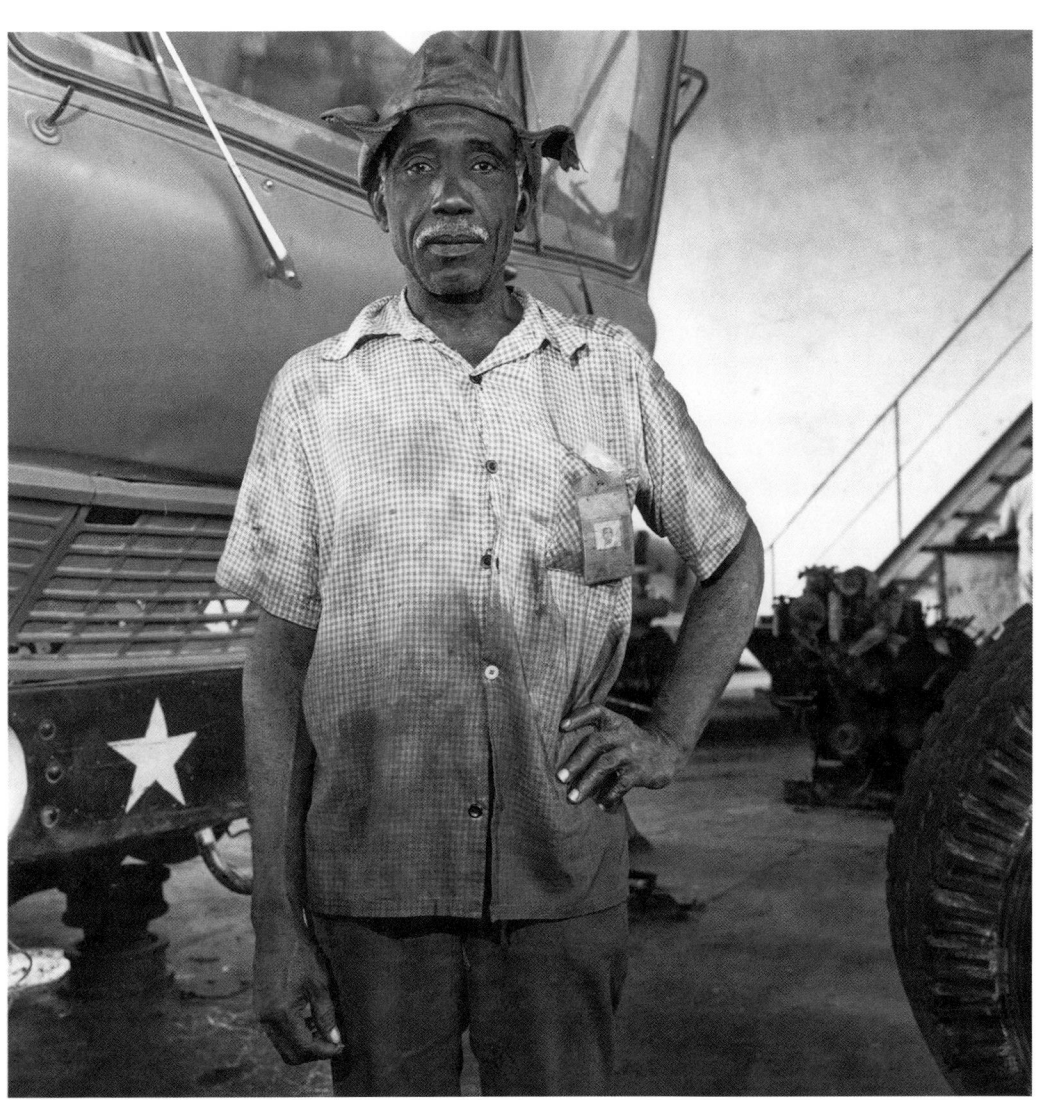

Restos del Coral Island

"Esa chatarra que se ve en la orilla
son los restos del *Coral Island*",
decía mi padre
hechizado por las columnas de luz blanca
que levitaban de los huecos rojizos
que tal vez sirvieron de anteojos
a la proa de ese gran trasatlántico
que dice mi padre era el *Coral Island*.
Vamos sentados en un ómnibus cotidiano,
rápido y caluroso como este mes de julio de 1986.
No quise preguntarle porque me dio un vuelco el corazón.
Un zumbido de mariposas también me impidió hacer
   preguntas.
Mi padre me miró de un modo peculiar.
¿Habíamos entrado los dos
a reconocernos en aquel himno del pasado?
Mi padre y yo mirándonos sin decir nada.
Yo sólo tenía oídos para escuchar el chirriar de las
   olas
contra los hierros tutelares del *Coral Island*.
Y pensé en una historia de amor,
en una pasión desmoronada sobre dientes de perro
   y espuma de mar.
Una loca pasíon bien muerta,
fenecida,
de la que ni siquiera se desprende ya
una columna de luz blanca
ni el portento a la vista que se llamó,
alguna vez, el *Coral Island*.
"Esa chatarra que se ve en la orilla
son los restos del *Coral Island*",
volvía a decir mi padre sin mirarme.

The Wreck of the Coral Island

"That wreck you see on the shore
is what's left of the *Coral Island*,"
my father used to say,
bewitched by the columns of white light
rising off the red-colored holes
through which a lookout may have gazed
on the bow of that great ocean liner
that my father says was the *Coral Island*.
We are sitting on the bus we take everyday,
it's fast and sweltering like this month of July, 1986.
He gave my heart such a jolt. I don't try to question him.
The blow of butterfly wings stopped my questions too.
My father gave me a strange look.
Had we both started
to recognize ourselves in that hymn from the past?
My father and I, looking at each other, not saying a word.
All my ears heard was the hissing of the waves
against the shackles holding fast the *Coral Island*.
And I thought about a love story,
about a passion worn away by rocks like fangs
     and ocean spray.
A crazy passion long dead,
over and done with,
a passion that no longer beams
a column of white light
nor wonder like the sight of what was called,
once upon a time, the *Coral Island*.
"That wreck you see on the shore
is what's left of the *Coral Island*,"
my father said again without looking at me.

(P.C.)

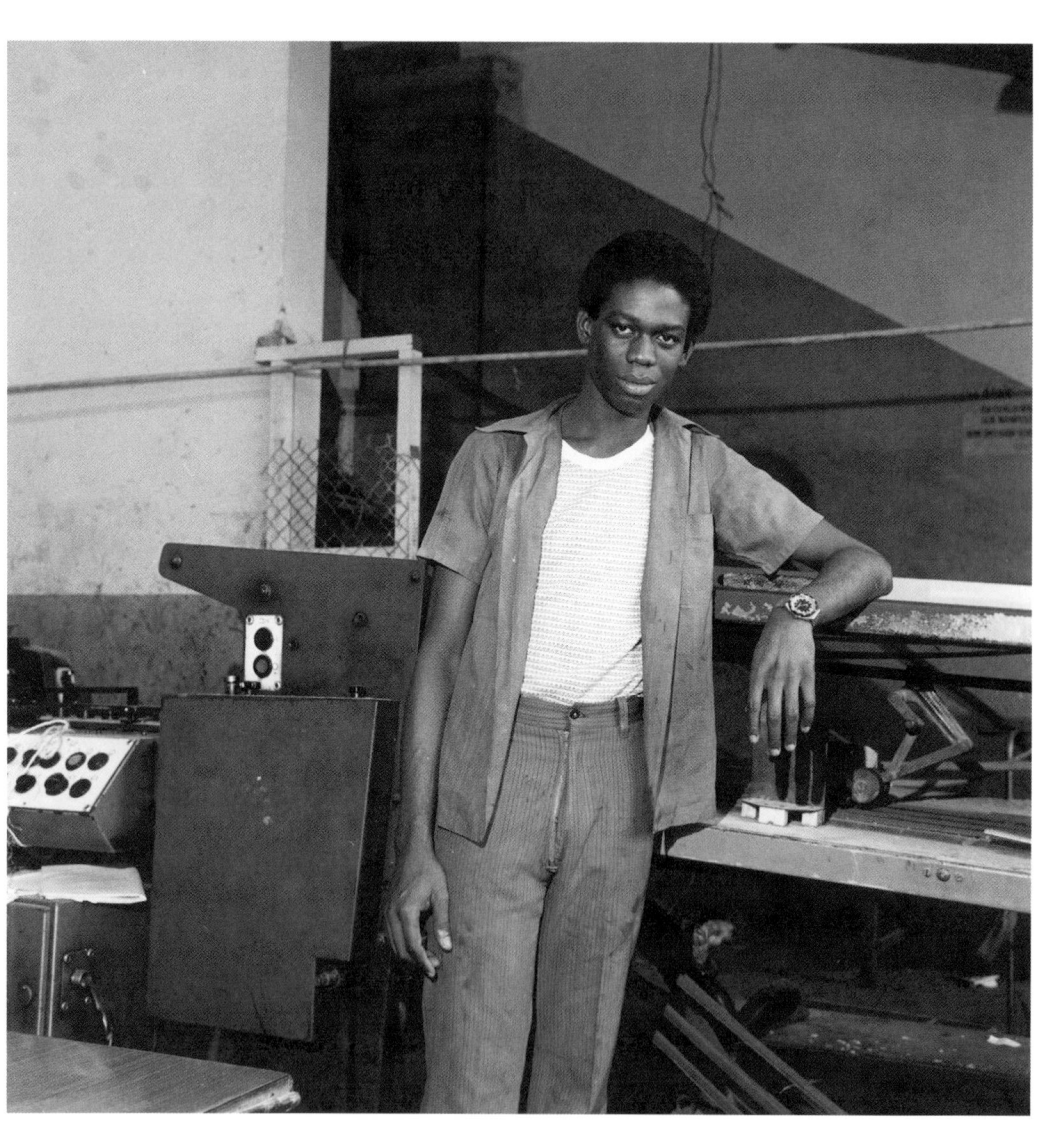

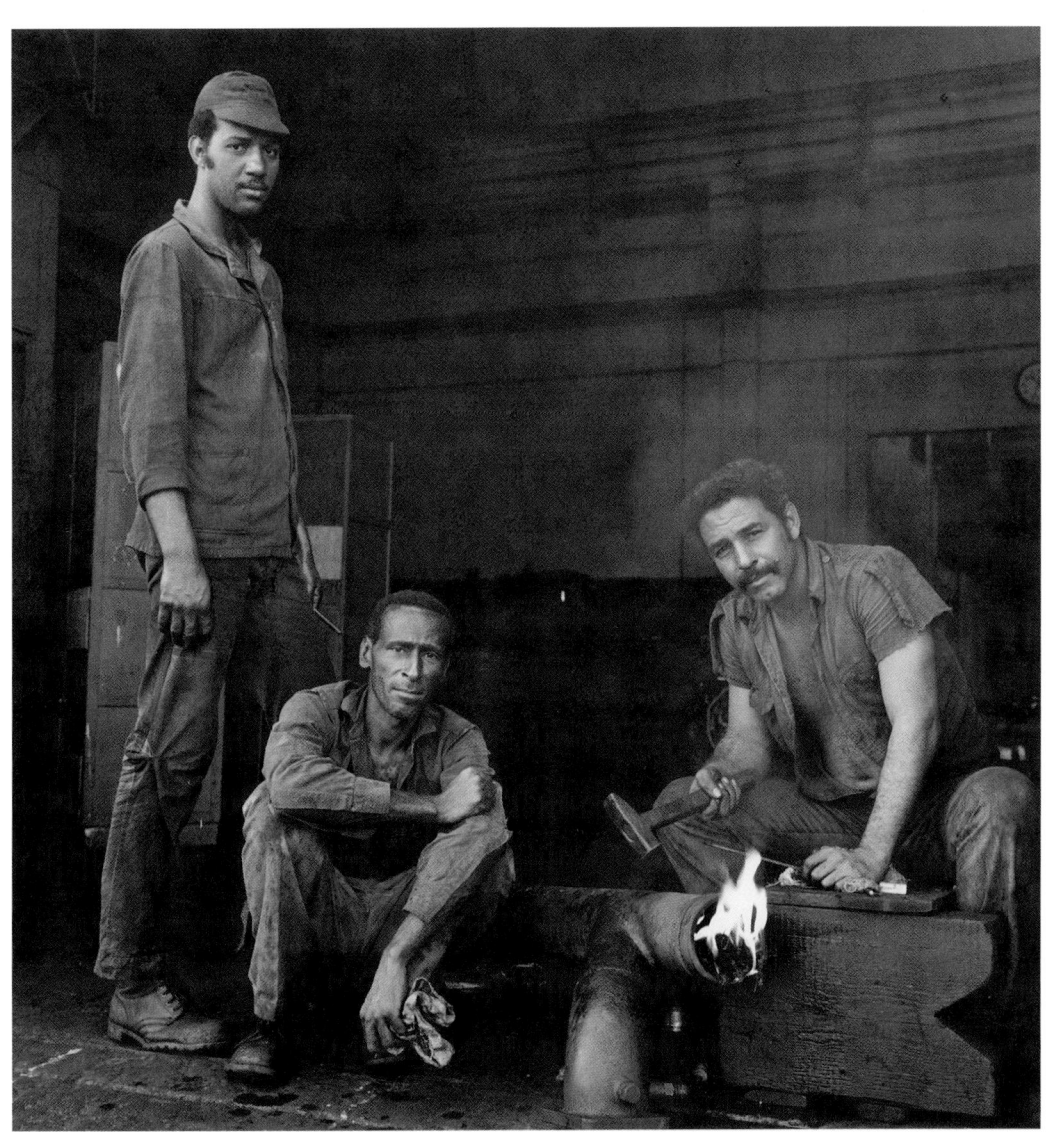

Y arderán las banderas

Y arderán las banderas como simples cernícalos.
Seremos el peso del universo, los mortales factores
y los materialistas de la creación.

And the Flags Will Burn

And the flags will burn like merest kestrels.
We will become the weight of the universe, the mortal factors,
the materialists of creation.

(D.F.)

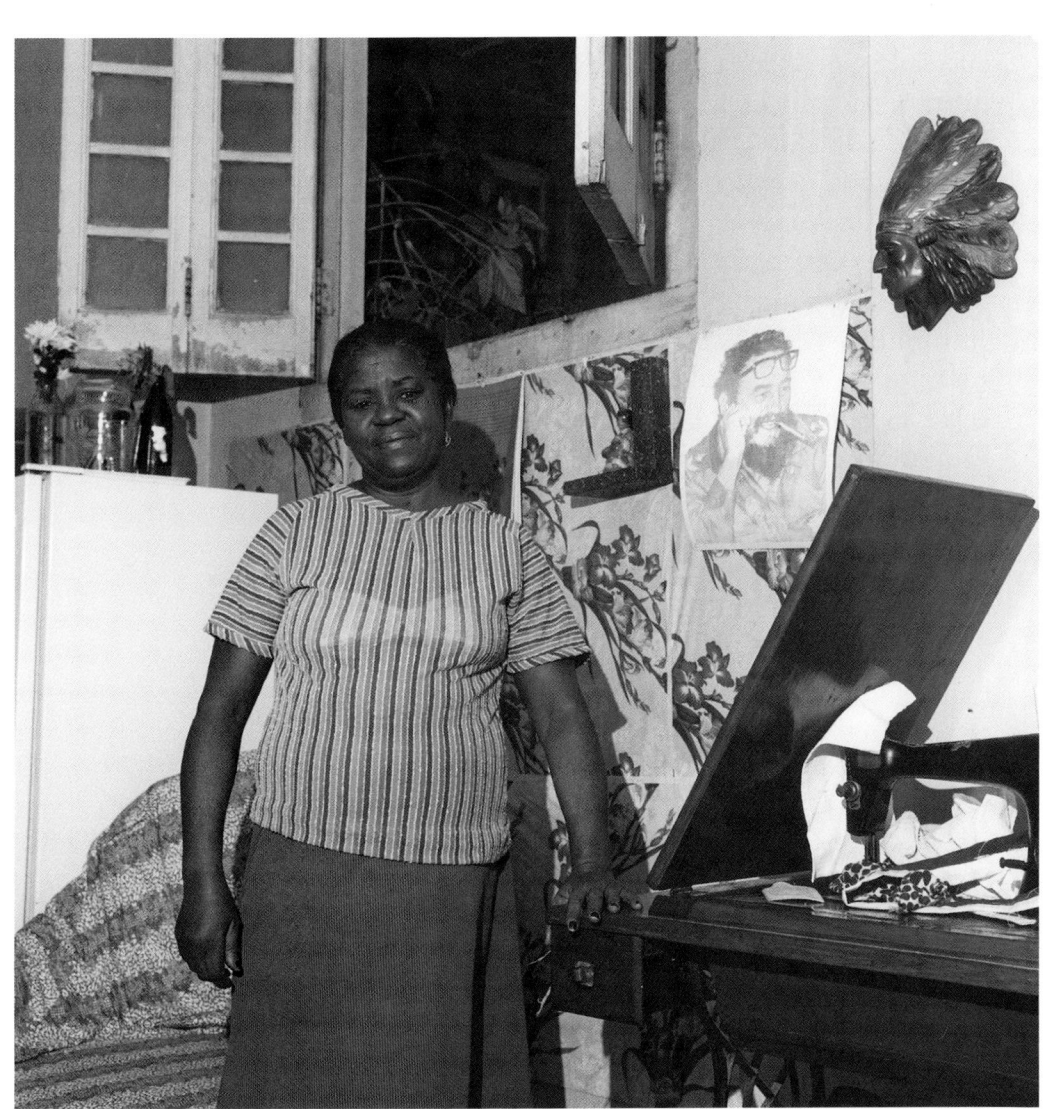

Mujeres nuevas

La flecha ecuatorial
perdida aún bajo los párpados.
Flores silvestres en el pecho,
quemadas por todos los salitres del mundo.
El trino del gallo en la montaña.
El silbido del humo en la ciudad.
Y sus manos, que vienen de muy lejos,
desde remotas eras,
amasando la sustancia reciente
que nos hace vivir
entre el mar y las costas,
entre los peces y las redes,
entre las ventanas y el horizonte.
Estas mujeres van alzando,
marchando,
cosiendo,
martillando,
tejiendo,
sembrando,
limpiando,
conquistando,
leyendo,
amando.
Oh, simples mujeres nuevas
simples mujeres negras
dando el aliento vivo
de una luz nueva
para todos.

New Women

The equator's arrow
lost even beneath their eyelids.
At their breast, wild flowers
burned by all the saltpeter in the world.
The crowing of the rooster in the mountain.
The whistle of smoke in the city.
And their hands, that come from so far away,
from by-gone times,
kneading together the yeasty substance
that makes us live
between the sea and the shores,
between fishes and nets,
between windows and the horizon.
These women go on rising,
marching,
sewing,
hammering,
knitting,
sowing,
cleaning,
conquering,
reading,
loving.
Oh, upright new women,
upright black women,
bringing the blessed breath
of a new light
for us all.

(P.C.)

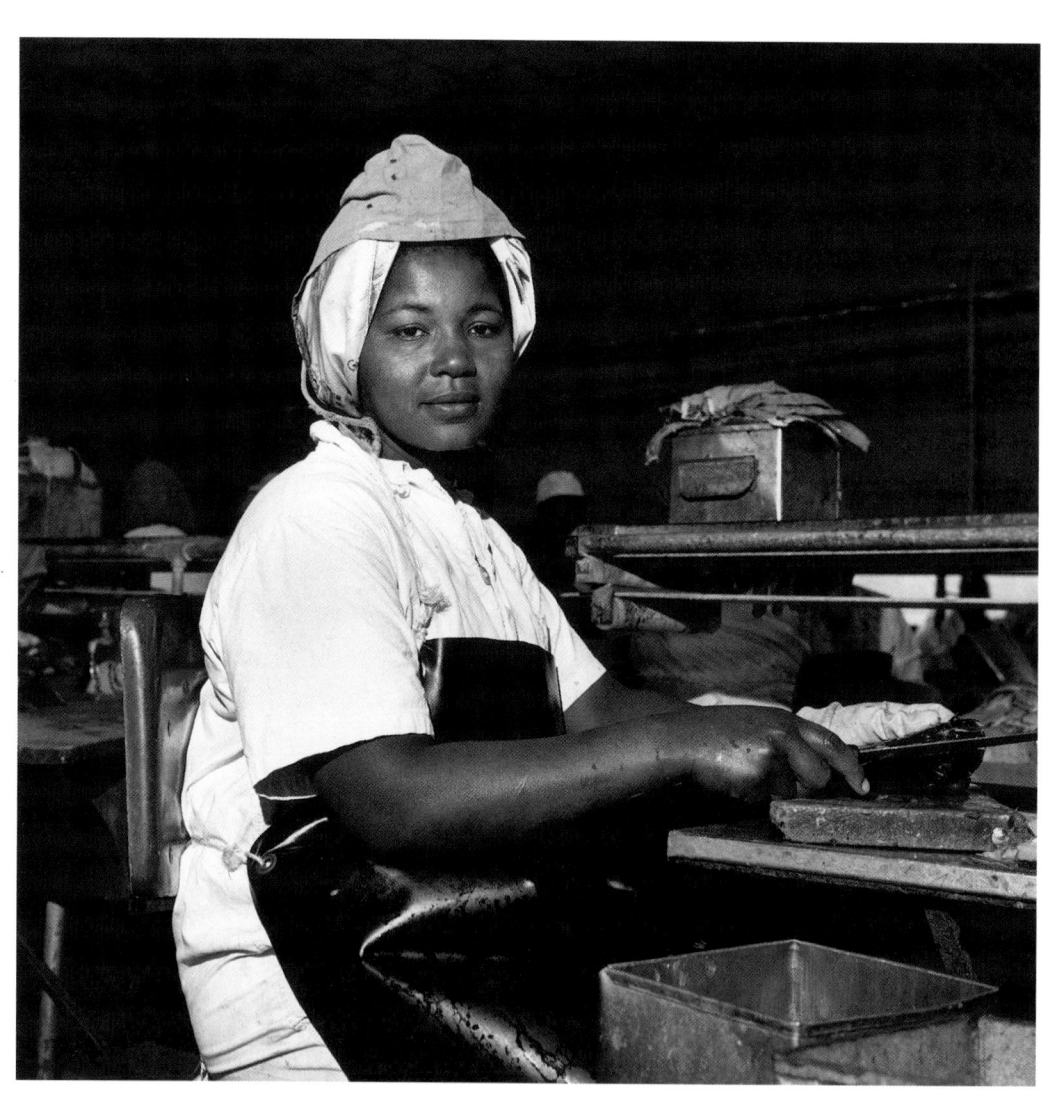

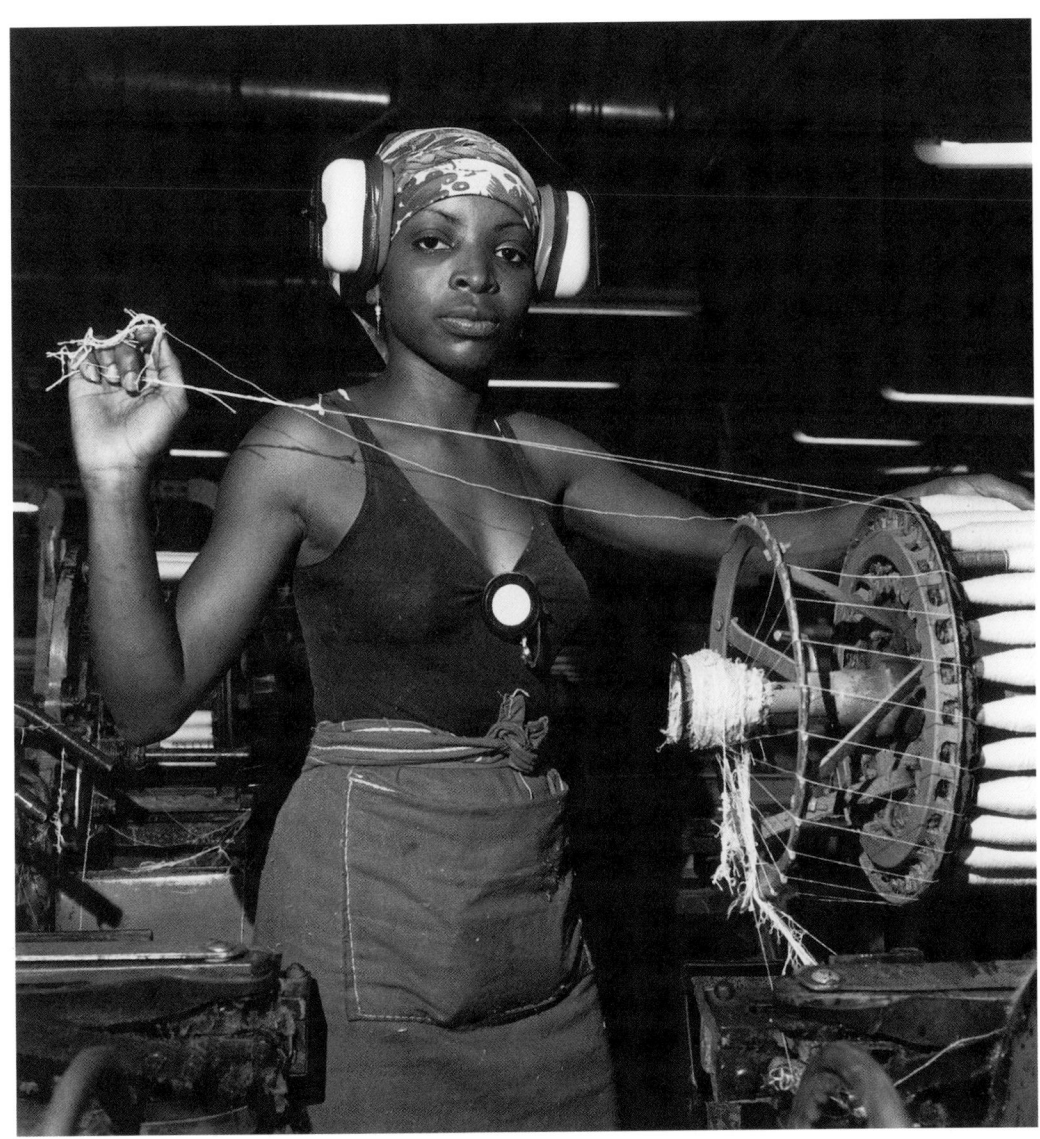

Nueva fábula de albañil

Entre arena y gravilla,
mezcla y paleta,
va transcurriendo su vida
que irradia cien mil vidas
en la fiereza del andamio
en donde nace su espalda peregrina,
tan dura como el ágata,
dispuesta a todo
para el porvenir.

The New Fable of the Bricklayer

Amid sand and fine gravel,
mortar and trowel,
his life unfolds
and beams down on a hundred thousand lives
from the fierce strength of the scaffold
where his pilgrim back is born,
hard as agate,
ready for everything
the future brings.

(P.C.)

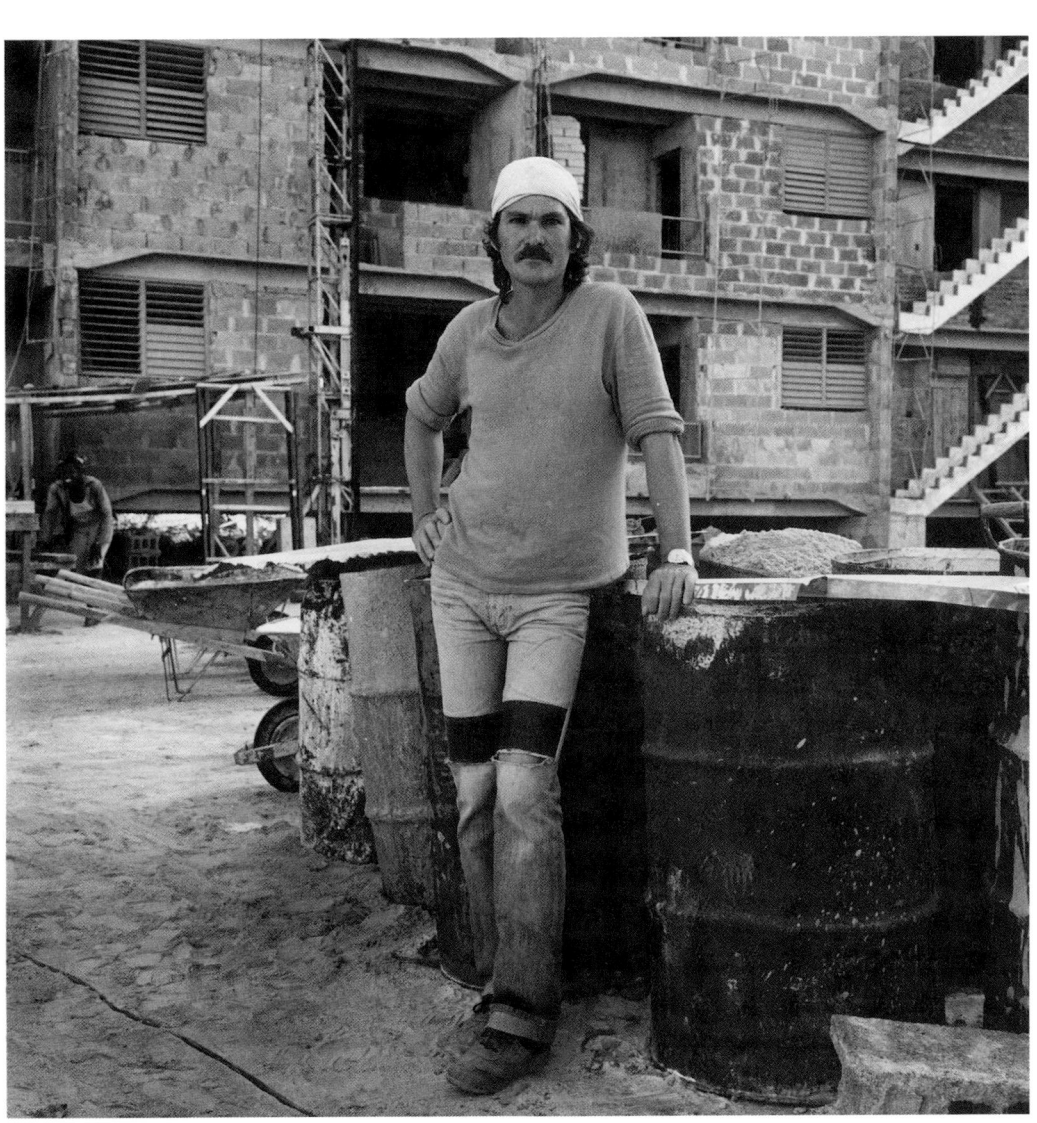

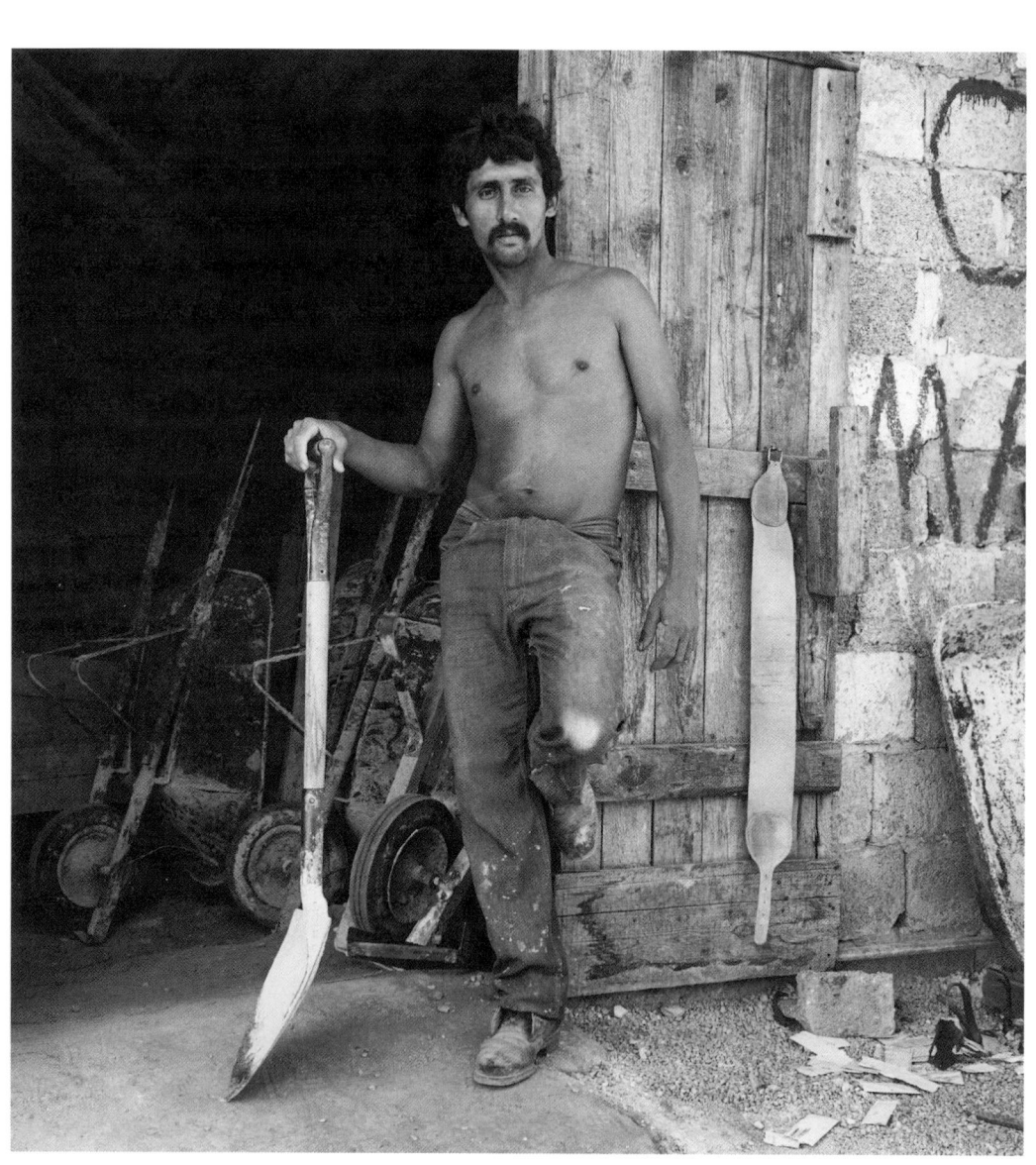

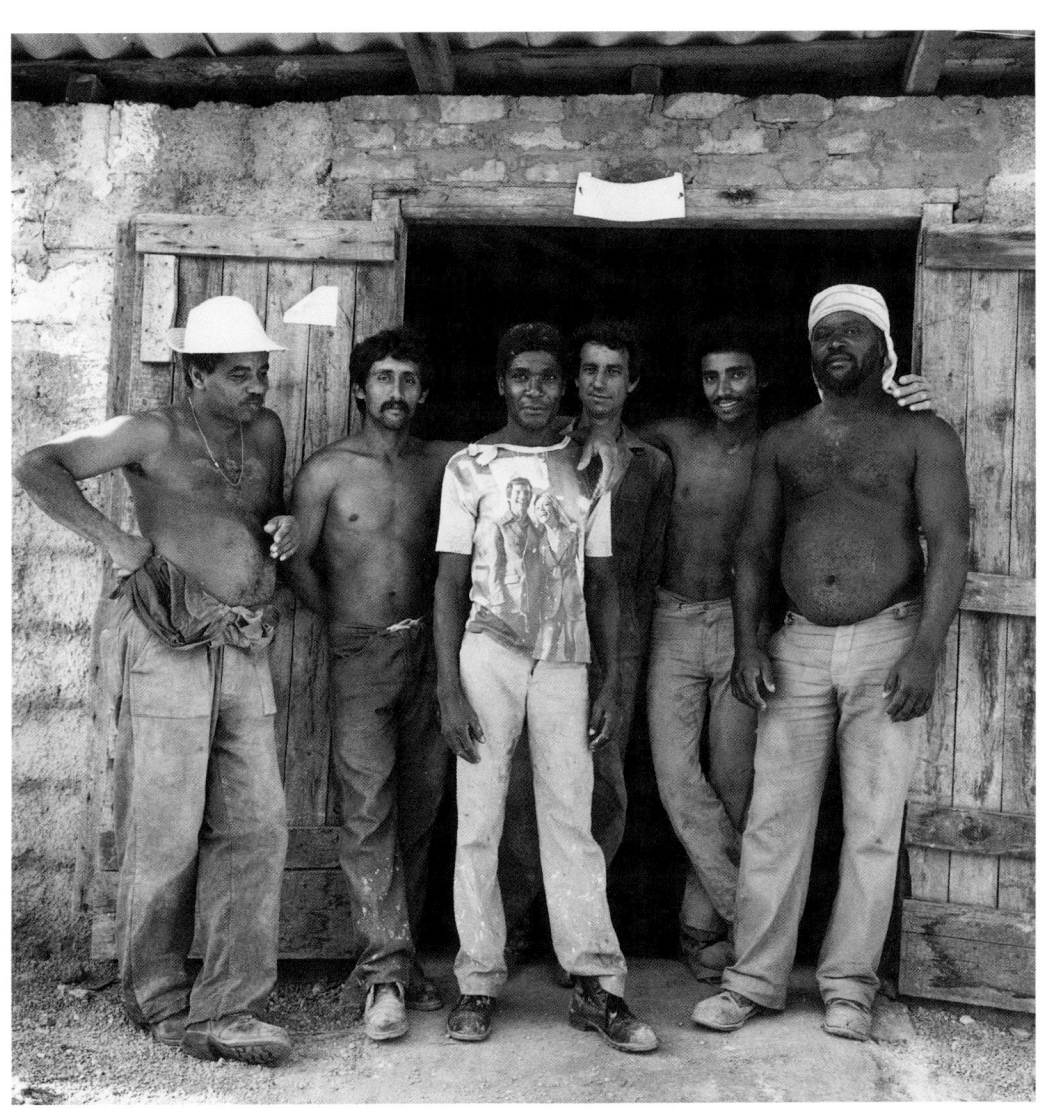

Haremos la vida

Esta es la existencia
y el sudor de quien erige el mundo, día tras día.
¡Alguna vez haremos la vida!

We Will Make A Life

This is how it is
and this is how we sweat while we're building the world, day by day.
One of these days we'll make ourselves a life!

(D.F.)

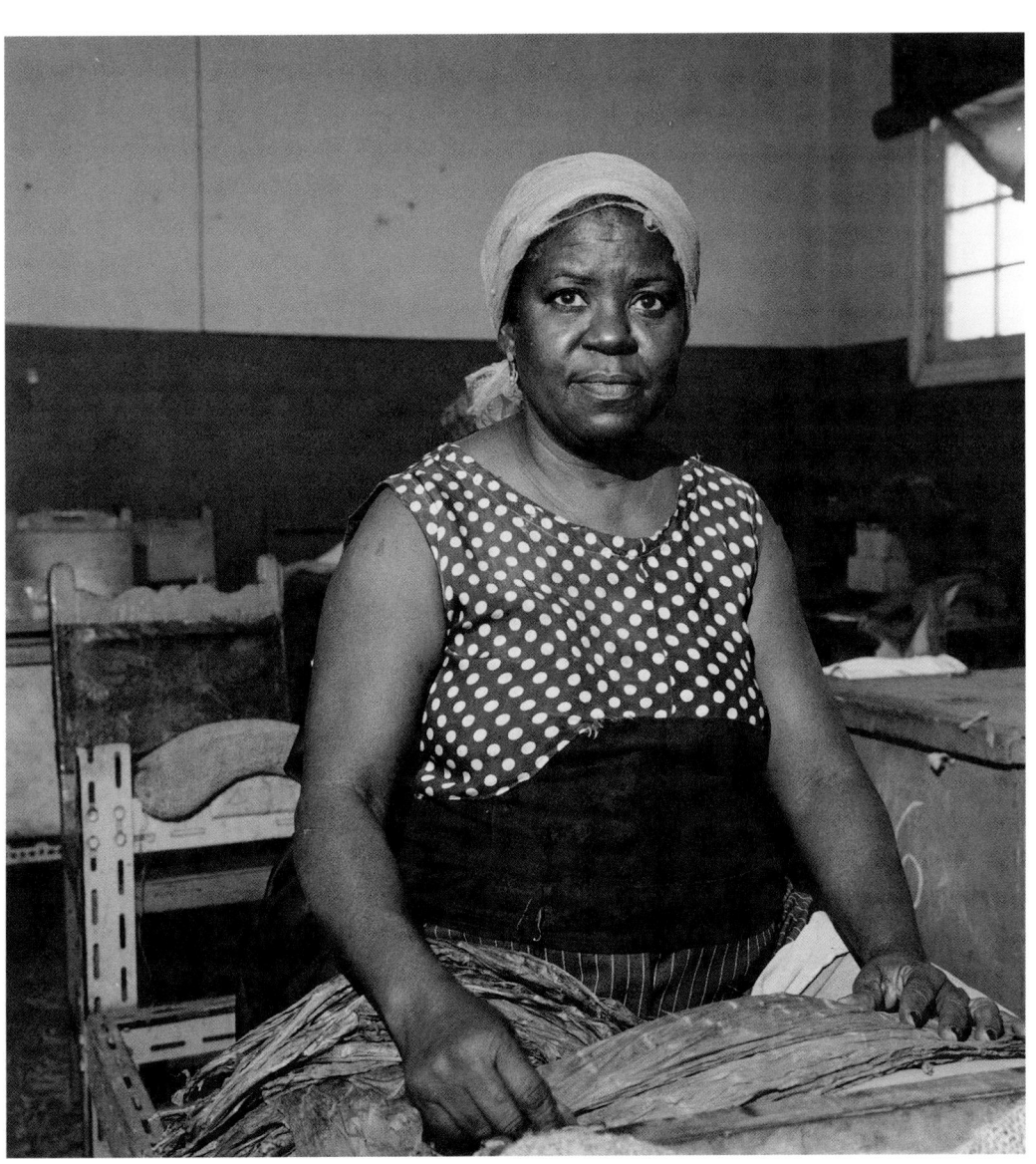

Obrera del tabaco

Una obrera del tabaco escribió
un poema a la muerte. Entre el humo
y las hojas torcidas y secas de la vega
dijo ver el mundo en Cuba.
Era el año 1999... En su poema
dijo tocar las flores
formadoras de una mágica alfombra
que circunvolaba la Plaza de la Revolución.
En su poema, esa obrera
palpó los días de la mañana.
En su poema, no había penumbras sino lámparas energéticas.
En su poema, amigos, no habia Miami ni reclamaciones;
no había mendicidad,
no había ruindades,
ni violaciones de la ley laboral;
no había interés por la Bolsa, no había lucro.
En su poema, había astucia militante, lánguida inteligencia
En su poema, había disciplina y asambleas.
En su poema, había sangre hirviendo del pasado.
En su poema, había higado y corazones.
Su poema era un tratado de economía popular.
En su poema, estaban todos los deseos y toda la ansiedad
de un revolucionario contemporáneo suyo.
Una obrera del tabaco escribió
un poema a la agonía del capitalismo. Sí, señor.
Pero ni sus hermanos, ni sus vecinos,
adivinaron la esencia de su vida. Y nunca supieron del poema.
Ella lo había guardado, tenaz y finamente,
junto a unas hojas de caña santa y cáñamo
dentro de un libro, empastado,
de José Martí.

Tobacco Worker

A tobacco worker wrote
a poem to death. Amid the smoke
and the dry and twisted leaves of the plains
she said she saw the world in Cuba.
It was the year 1999... In her poem
she said she touched the flowers
that formed a magic carpet
flying circles round the Plaza of the Revolution.
In her poem, this worker
grasped tomorrow's days.
In her poem there were no half shadows, just energetic lamps.
In her poem, friends, there was no Miami, no claims being made;
there was no begging,
there were no acts of malice,
no violations of the labor law;
there was no interest in the Stock Exchange, there was no profit.
Her poem was full of militant cunning, languid intelligence.
Her poem was full of discipline and meetings.
Her poem was full of guts and heart.
Her poem was a treatise on popular economy.
Her poem was full of the desires and anxieties
of a revolutionary, her contemporary.
A tobacco worker wrote
a poem to the death throes of capitalism. Yes, sir.
But not even her brothers, not even her neighbors
guessed at the essence of her life. And they never learned of the poem.
She had kept it, tenaciously and delicately,
together with some leaves of hemp and *caña santa*,
in a clothbound book
of José Martí.

(D.F.)

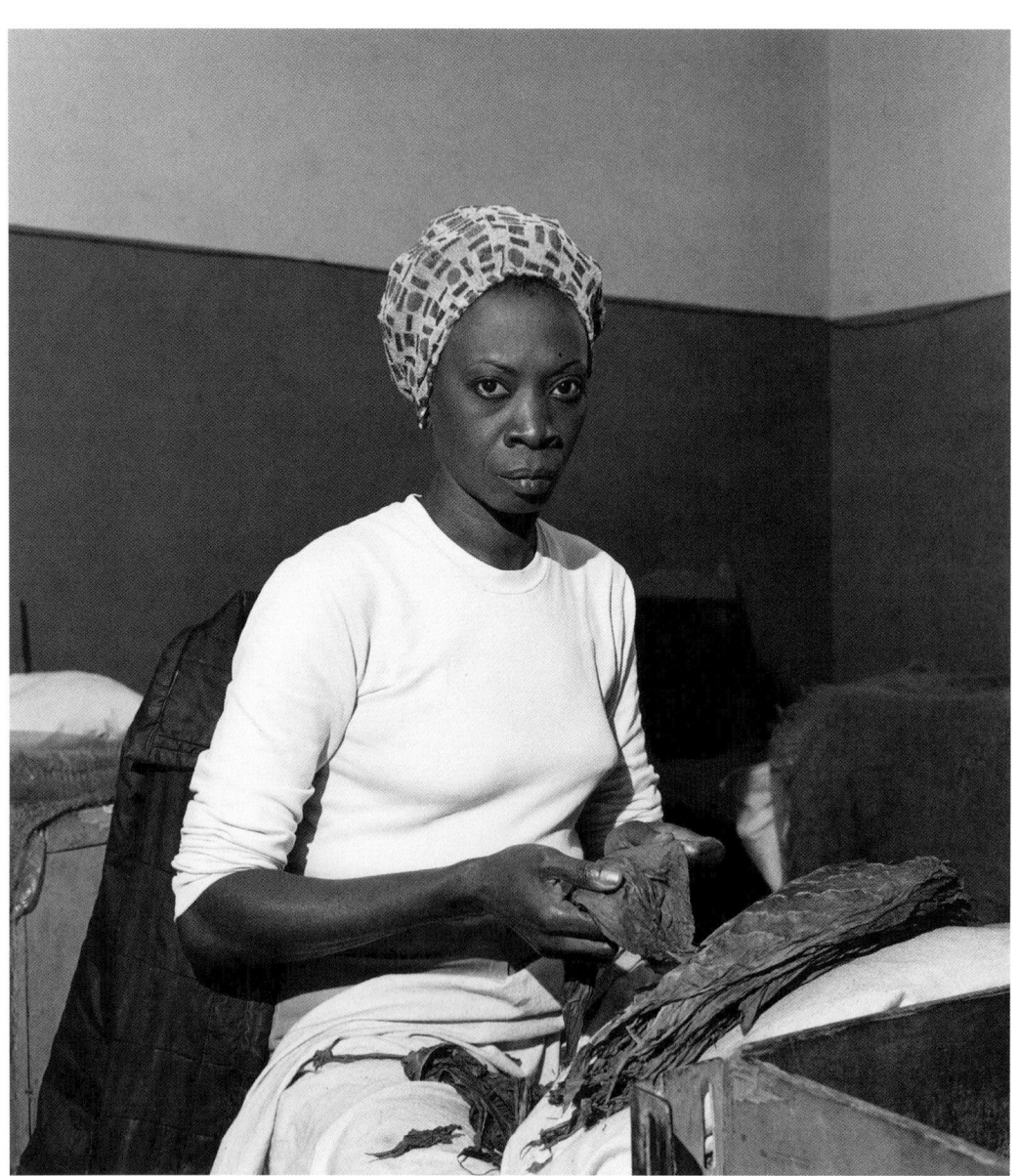

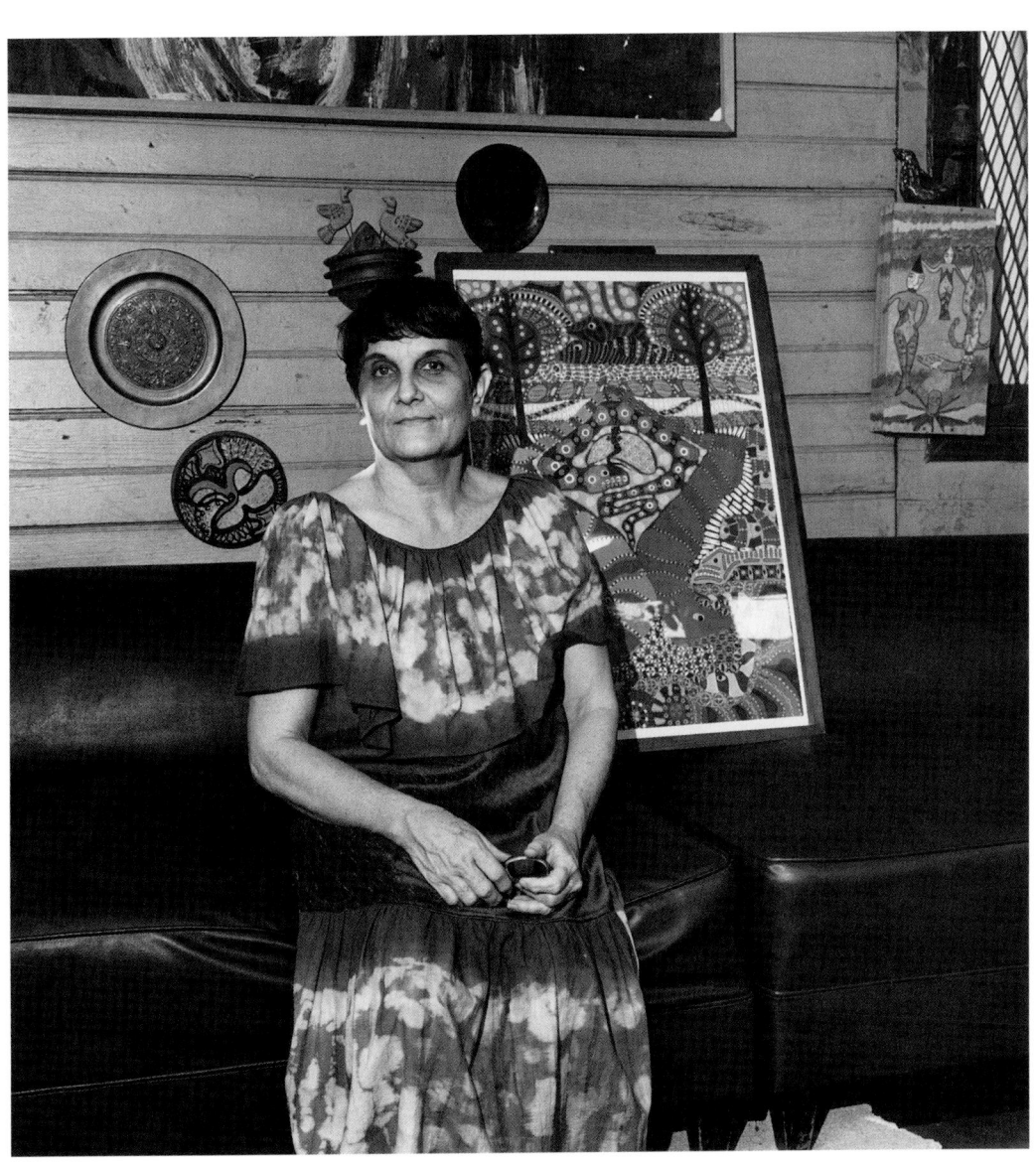

Antonia Eiriz

Antonia Eiriz
hizo palpables
los sueños en la noche.
Echó a volar
animalillos y sirenas
en medio del atardecer.
Pobló la isla de muñecos sin fin
y los hizo rodar entre los barrios
con amena nostalgia.
Sus pinceles son un ejemplo vivo
de tinta y de papel y aquí están
para hablarnos de la mañana.
Antonia Eiriz sonríe
y el flautista de Hamelin
ya la viene a buscar
los dos saltan, saltan,
como dos buenos reyes
frente a su ejército encantado.
Antonia Eiriz dibuja
para todas las aves del lugar.

Antonia Eiriz

Antonia Eiriz
made our nighttime dreams
come to life.
She set free
little animals and mermaids
as the sun was setting.
She stocked our island with no end of puppets
and sent them tumbling down our streets
with pleasant nostalgia.
Her brushes show how alive ink and paper
can be and they're here
to tell us about the morning.
Antonia Eiriz laughs
and the Pied Piper of Hamelin
comes at once to find her
and the two of them jump and leap
like two good kings
leading their enchanted army.
Antonia Eiriz draws
for all the birds in town.

(P.C.)

Alquimia

Amas la libertad
y no sólo su nombre.
La libertad es como una paloma
aparecida en el umbral
de una puerta entreabierta
que no escucha el silencio
precipitado del abismo.
Amas la libertad
y no sólo su idea.
La libertad es como otra paloma
volando hacia el azul
sin miedo a los ciclones.

Asomarse a estos talleres rústicos,
de estables peregrinos,
es contemplar la libertad en alto grado.
Sus manos tejen la vieja alquimia
de las palomas mensajeras
y el yeso y los papeles
fundan un nuevo reino
de máscaras y ensueños.
Amas la libertad y no sólo su nombre.
¡Qué libertad la de estas manos
dueñas de su destino!

Alchemy

You love freedom
and not just its name.
Freedom is like a dove
that appears on the threshold
of a half-opened door
and pays no heed to the silence
streaming from the abyss.
You love freedom
and not just the idea of it.
Freedom is like another dove
flying out into the blue
with no fear of cyclones.

To peer out of those crude workshops
that belong to steadfast pilgrims,
is to gaze upon freedom at its purist.
Their hands spin the old alchemy
of carrier pigeons,
and their plaster and papers
merge, founding a new kingdom
of masks and daydreams.
You love freedom
and not just its name.
Masters of their destiny,
these hands have such freedom!

(P.C.)

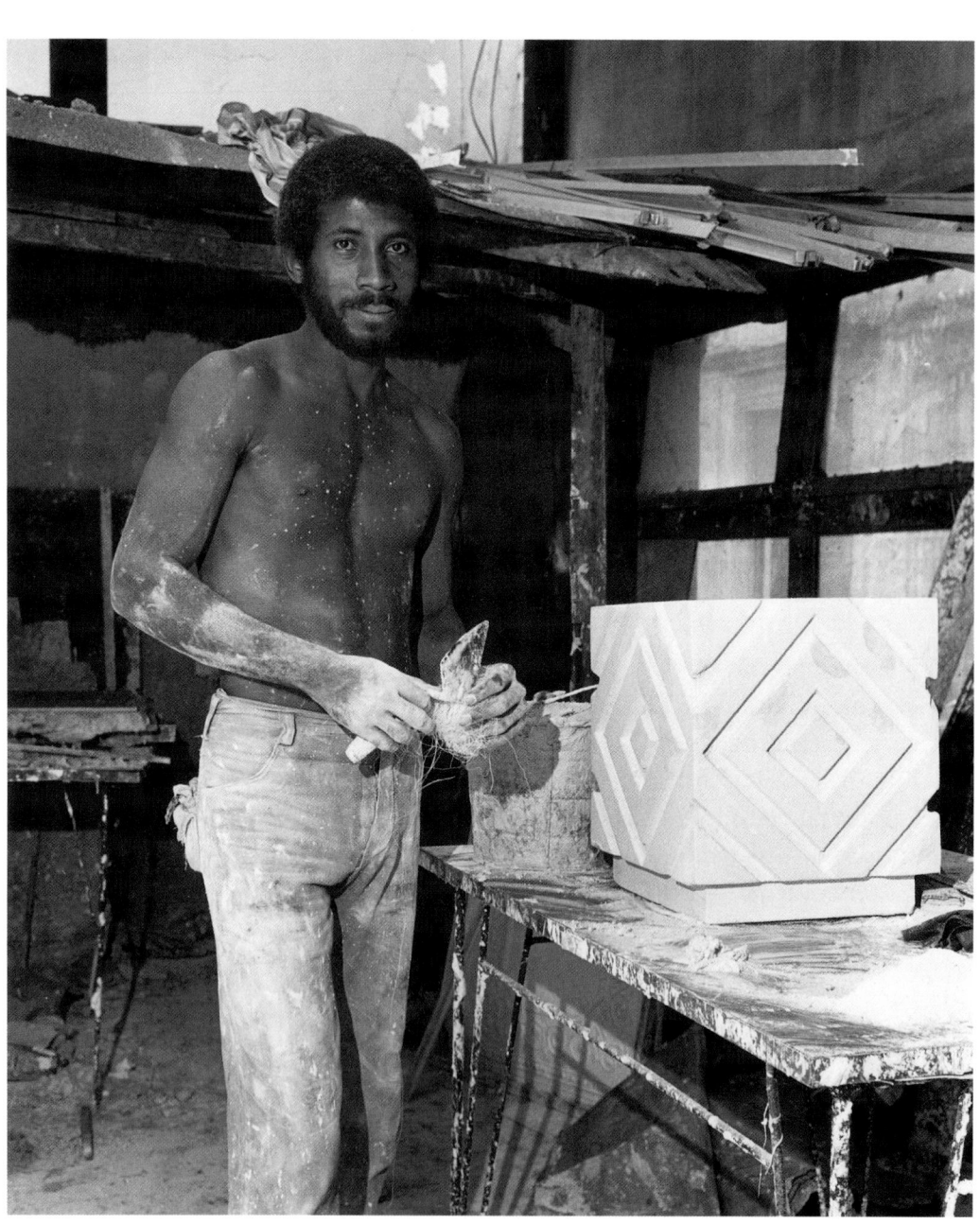

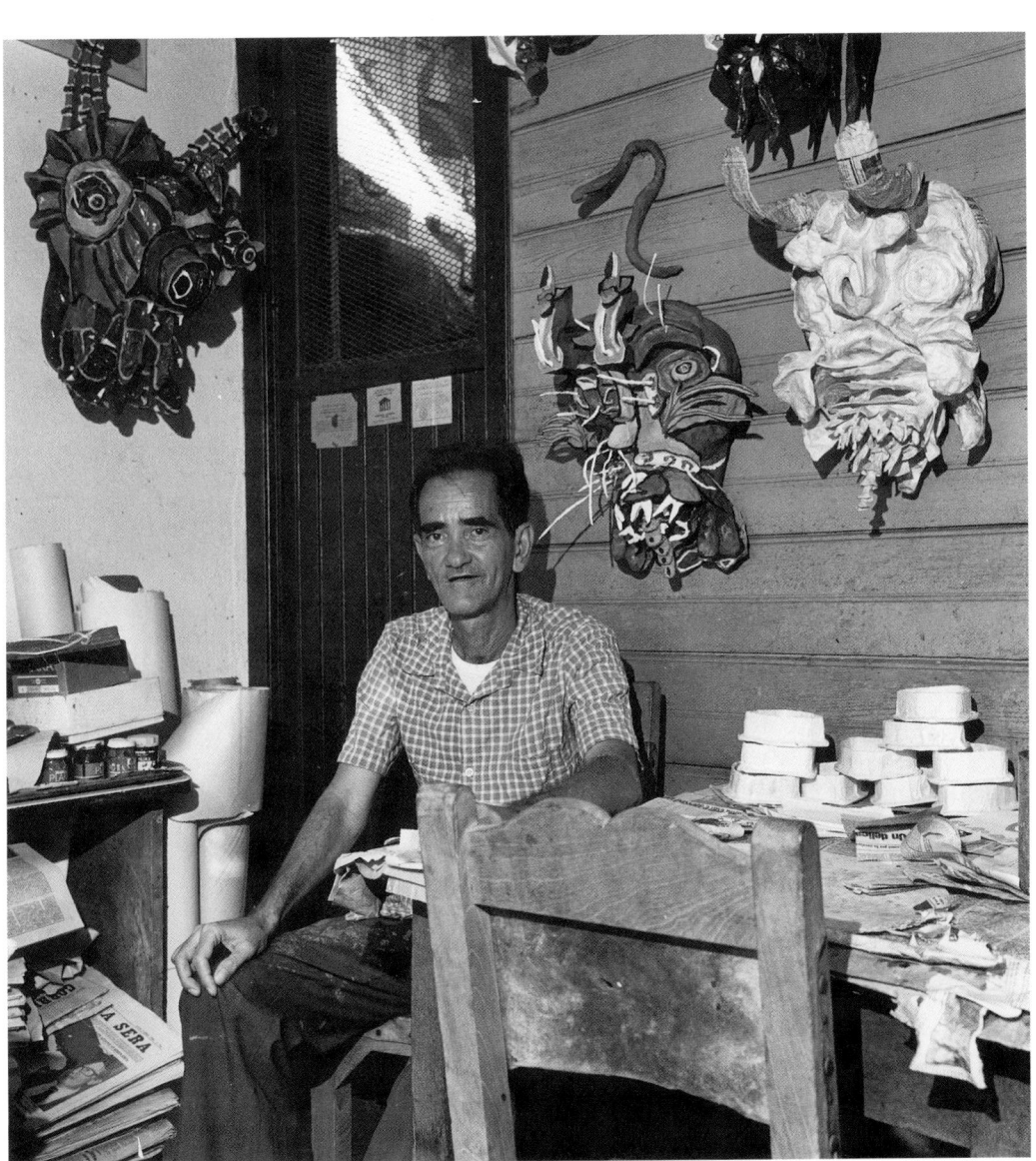

Los artesanos

A la memoria de Lidia Lavallée

Lidia, mira
esas manos, tan sabias e industriosas,
que componen con hilos, rosas y papeles
esos mundos preciosos que tú nos enseñaste a descubrir,
hasta quererlos y necesitarlos todos los días.
Lidia,
donde quiera que estés,
con tu pamela única,
mira estas criaturas sin afeites, hechas de pompa y voluntad,
flotando en el silencio de la madrugada,
entre el aroma fiero de las comparsas,
sobre los techos citadinos de Ayestarán
y el polvo del Juanelo.
Lidia,
¿cómo has podido dejarnos
tanta belleza,
tanta felicidad urbana
si no estás tú
sino en las curvas finas
que redondean los dedos de los artesanos
que aman la cábala y la piedrafina?
Lidia, ¿será posible?

The Artisans

> *In memory of Lidia Lavallée*

Lidia, look
at those hands, so wise and hard-working,
with threads, roses and papers they form
those precious worlds you taught us to discover,
even love them and need them every day.
Lidia,
wherever you are,
in your signature picture hat
look at these creatures, made of pomp and dedication,
waiting for paint,
floating in the silence of dawn,
amid the fierce aromas of *carnaval*,
above the city roofs of Ayestarán Street
and dust from Juanelo, our friend's hometown.
Lidia,
how could you have left us
such beauty,
such urbane happiness
if you aren't here
except in the delicate curves
smoothed out by the fingers of the artisans
who love the cabala and polished stones?
Lidia, how can this be?

(P.C.)

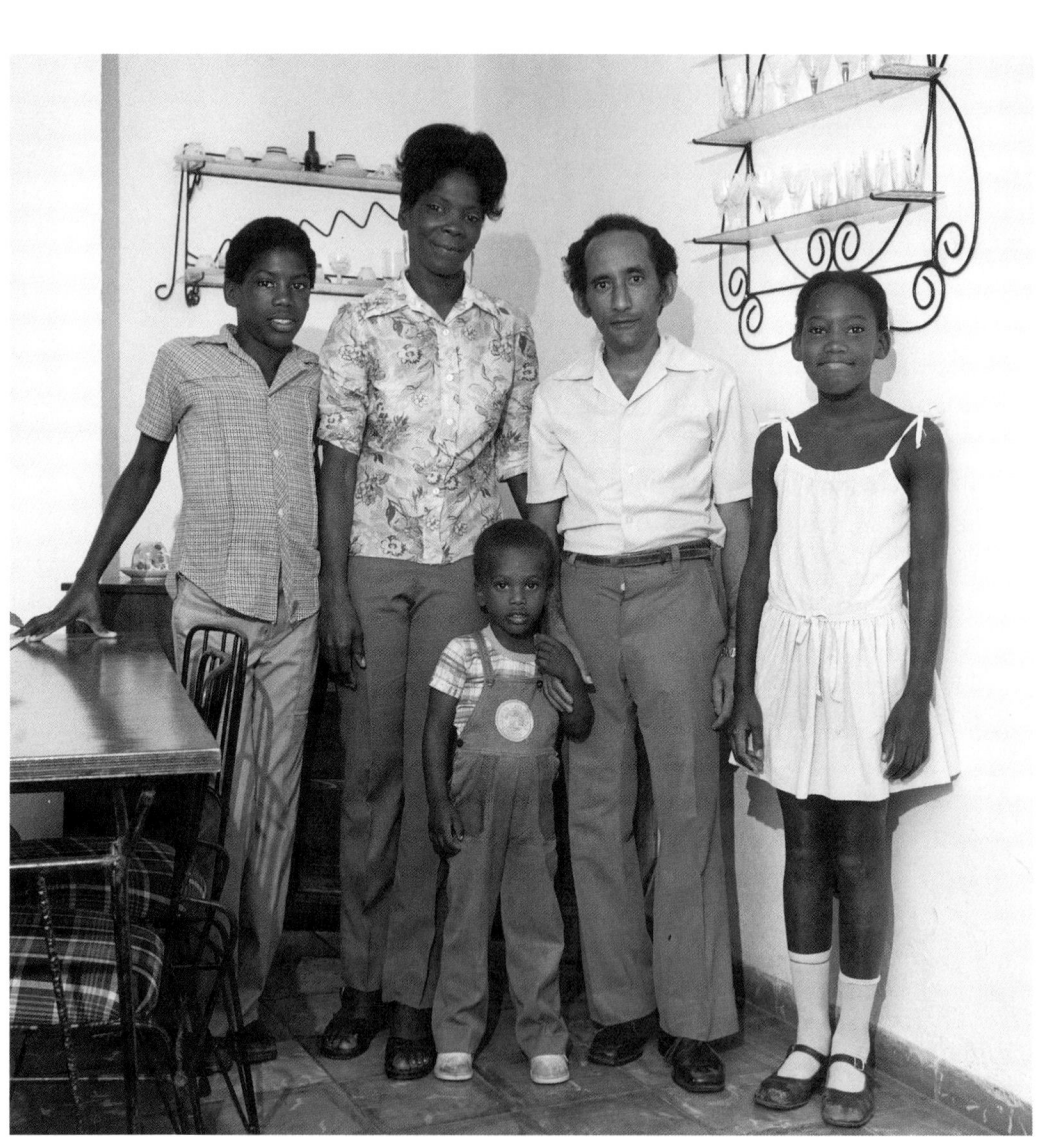

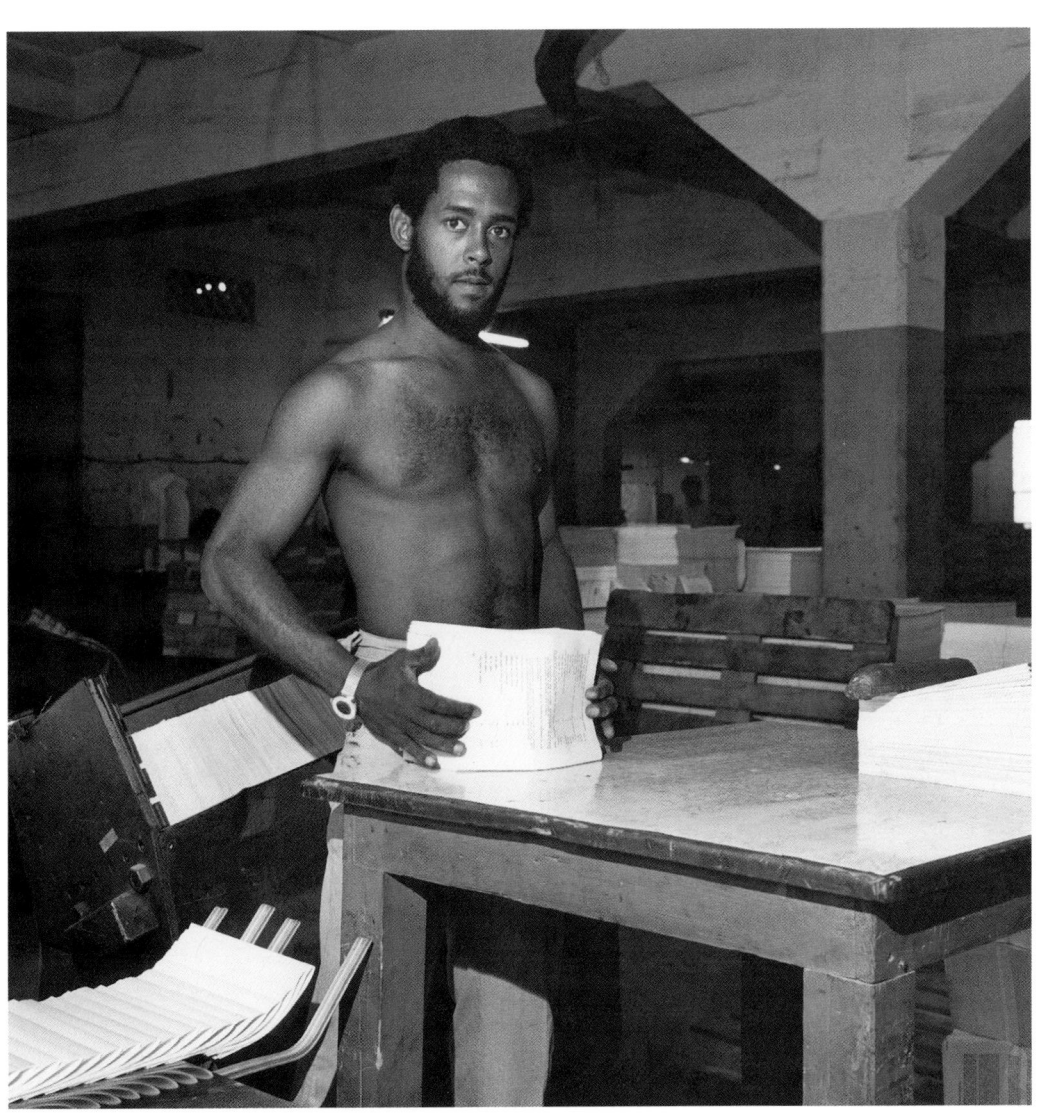

Cerco

Cercado por Bodonis, corondeles,
pliegos y guillotinas,
este joven detiene la faena
como buscando su quietud
entre tanto rumor.
La poesía del papel
lo ha subyugado tanto
que por eso nos está contemplando
en plenitud de vida.

Siege

Besieged by Bodonis, reglets,
folios and guillotines,
this young man halts his labor
as if searching for some quiet
amid all the racket.
The poetry of the paper
has him firmly in its grasp,
that's why he is taking stock of us
in the prime of his life.

(P.C.)

Note: Bodoni is a typeface; a reglet is a flat piece of wood used to seperate lines of handset type.

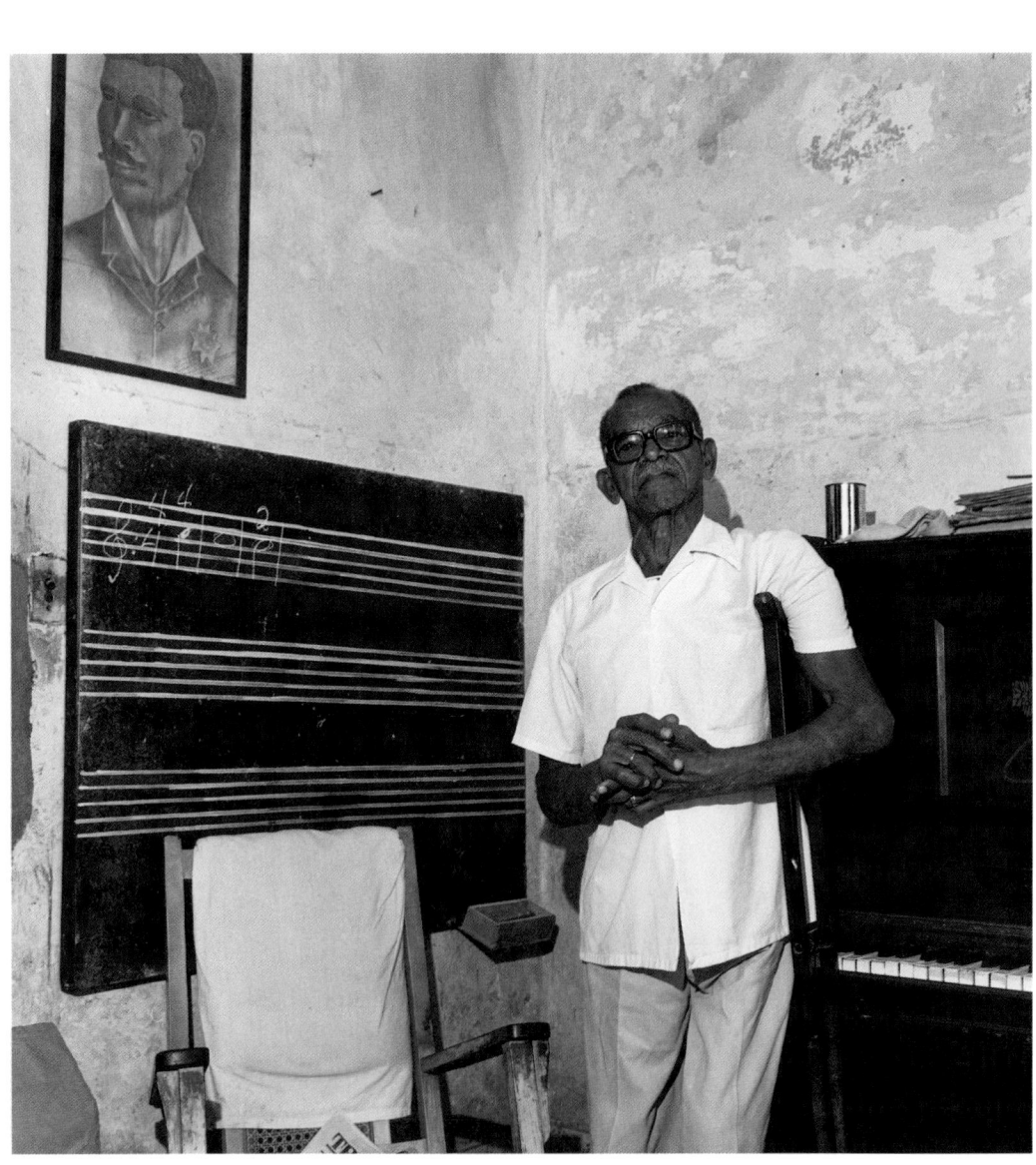

Patria

Este sillón enlaza en sus adentros
los dulces aires del violín
y los compases de la cajita china,
en fin, la melodía del danzón
en los atardeceres de domingo.
El perfume de Brindis de Salas
iba flotando también en la manigua
temblando como el corazón de la patria.

Homeland

Deep down, this rocking chair brings together
the sweet airs of the violin
and the drumming of the little chinese box,
all in all, the melody of the *danzon*
on late Sunday afternoons.
The fragrance of Brindis de Salas' music
floated on that jungle, too,
trembling like the heart of my homeland.

(P.C.)

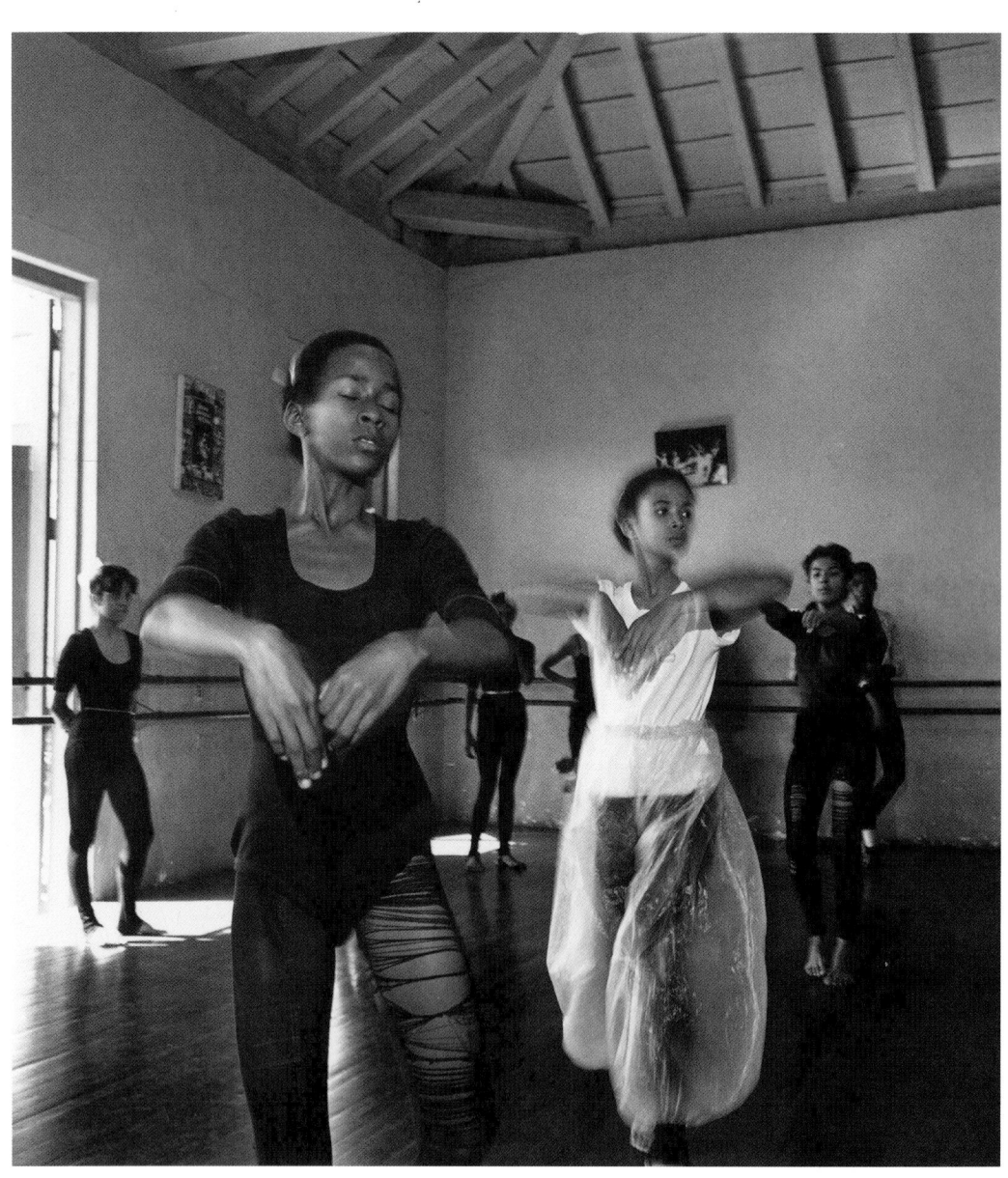

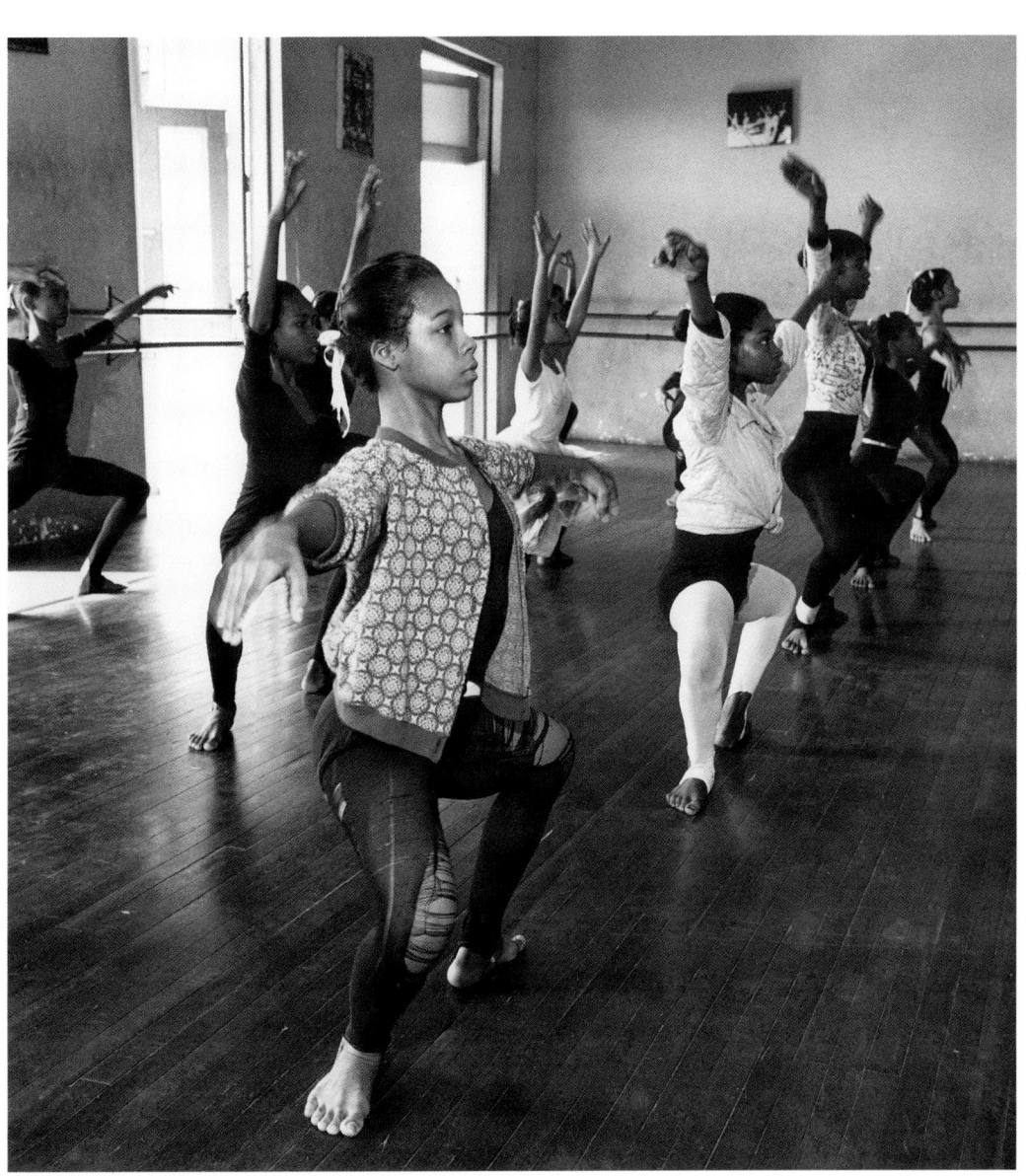

Elogio de la danza

Para Leo Brouwer

El viento sopla
como un niño
y los aires jadean
en la selva, en el mar.

Entras y sales
con el viento,
soplas la llama fría:
Velos de luna
soplas tú
y las flores y el musgo
van latiendo en el viento.

Y el cuerpo
al filo del agua,
al filo del viento,
en el eterno signo de la danza.

In Praise of Dance

For Leo Brouwer

The wind blows
like a child
and the breezes pant
on the jungle, on the sea.

You enter and leave
with the wind,
you blow on the cold flame:
You blow on
the veils of the moon,
and the flowers and the moss
are flapping in the wind.

And the body
at the edge of the storm,
at the edge of the wind,
in the eternal symbol of the dance.

(D.F.)

Elogio de las pequeñas bailarinas

Todo el pasado renace en estas pequeñas
bailarinas. Ellas, tal vez, no lo sospechan
ni siquiera la adviertan. Toda la fuerza de sus
ancestros revive en estas pequeñas bailarinas.
Bailar, girar, saltar al compás de todas
las victorias que hicieron posible que estas
pequeñas bailarinas labren su propio destino entre
los aires elevándose, en su genio, más allá
del percance y de una malla descosida. Toda la
danza estalla en estas pequeñas bailarinas
como una magia sagrada que nos asegura la perpetuidad
del arte entre los hombres. Todo el futuro renace en
estas pequeñas bailarinas.

In Praise of These Young Dancers

All the past is born again in these young
dancers. They do not suspect it, perhaps
do not even notice. All the strength of their
ancestors lives on again in these young girls.
Dancing, twirling, leaping to the beat of all
the victories that have allowed these
young dancers to carve out their own fates among
the winds, soaring, in their genius, far above
missteps and a pair of tattered tights. All the dance
bursts forth in these young dancers
like sacred magic, assuring us that art
will live forever among men. All the future is born again
in these young dancers.

(D.F.)

La cena

a mis padres

ha llegado el tío juan con su sombrero opaco
sentándose y contando los golpes
que el mar y los pesados sacos han propagado
por su cuerpo robusto

yo entro de nuevo a la familia
dando las buenas tardes
y claveteando sobre cualquier objeto viejo

sigo sin mirar fijamente
tomando el animal entre mis manos
distraída
pidiendo con urgencia los ojos de mi madre
como el agua de todos los días

papá llega más tarde
con sus brazos oscuros y sus manos callosas
enjuagando el sudor en la camisa simple
que amenaza dulzona con destrozar mis hombros
ahí está el padre
acurrucado casi
para que yo encontrara vida
y pudiera existir allí donde no estuvo
me detengo ante la gran puerta
y pienso
en la guerra que podría estallar súbitamente
pero veo a un hombre que construye
otro que pasa cuaderno bajo el brazo
y nadie
nadie podrá con todo esto

Supper

> *for my parents*

here comes uncle juan in his dark hat
sitting down to tell of the bruises
that the sea and heavy sacks have left
upon his robust body

i enter the family again
greeting everyone
and staring at any ancient object

i continue to avert my gaze
picking up the family pet
distracted
urgently yearning for my mother's gaze
like our daily water

papa comes in later on
with his dark arms and calloused hands
wiping his sweat off with his plain shirt
that sweetly threatens to ruin the shoulders of my blouse
there is the father
all but doubled over
so that i might find life
and could exist where he has never been
i stop before the big door
and think
about the war that could suddenly break out
but i see one man building
and another passing by notebook under arm
and no one
no one can handle all this

ahora
vamos todos temblorosos y amables
a la mesa
nos miramos más tarde
permanecemos en silencio
reconocemos que un intrepido astro
        desprende
de las servilletas de las tazas de los cucharones
        el olor a cebolla
de todo ese mirar atento y triste de mi madre
que rompe el pan inaugurando la noche

now
let's all go trembling and friendly
to the table
we look at each other later
we sit in silence
we see that a fearless star
falls off
from the napkins from the cups from the ladles
from the smell of onion
from all the attentive sad watchfulness of my mother
breaking bread inaugurating the evening

(D.F.)

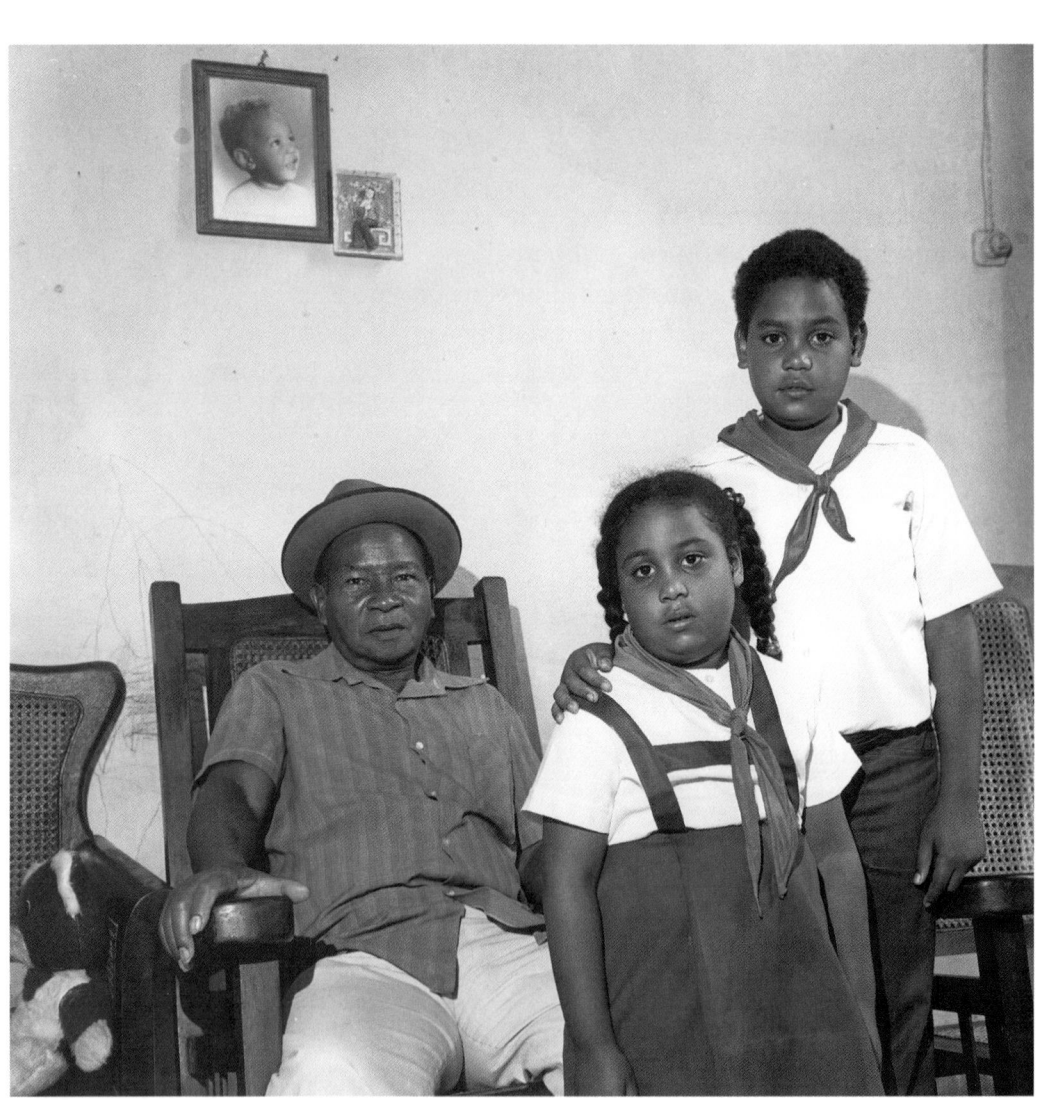

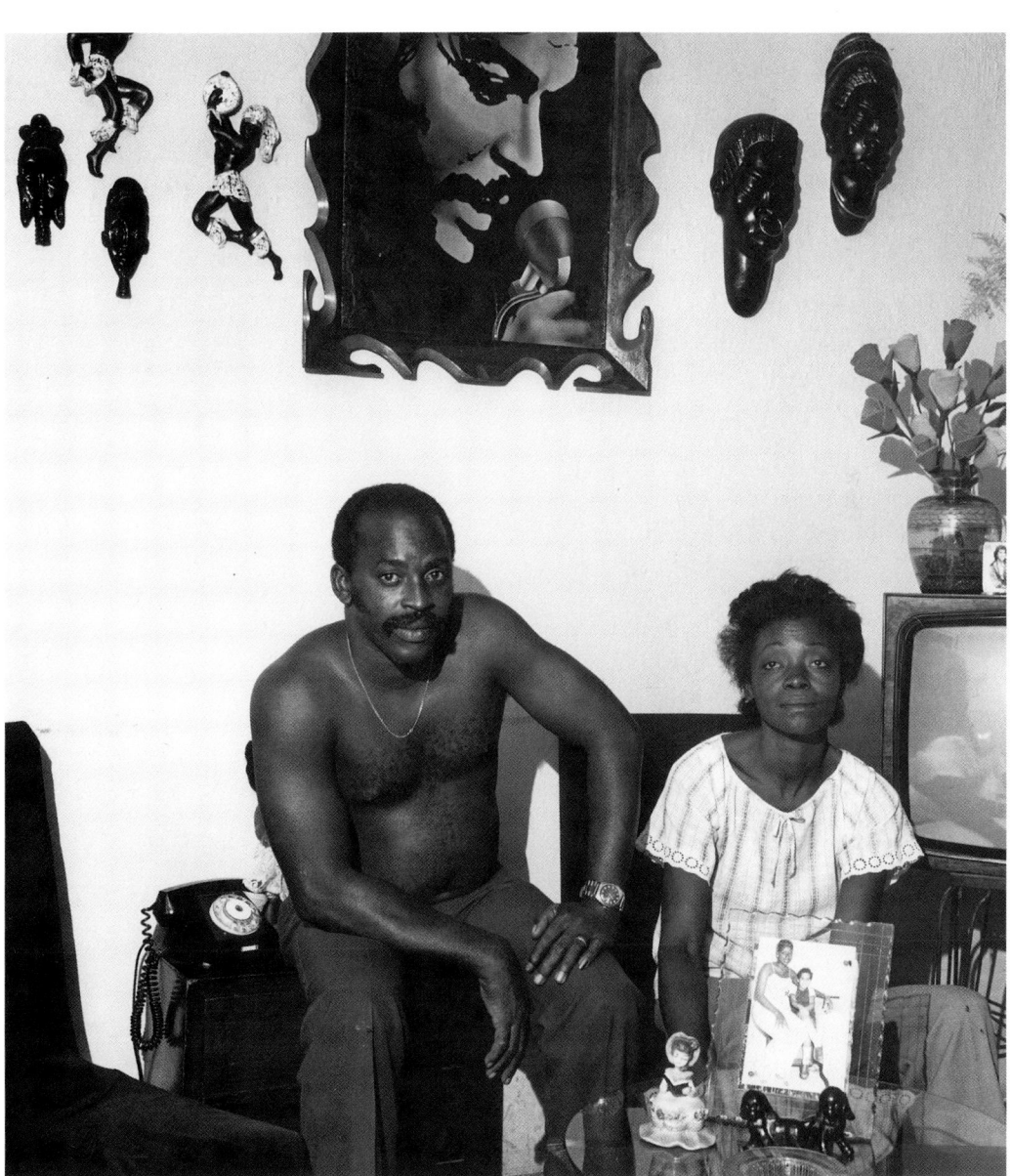

Pareja negra

Pasos en el océano
con ansias de baobab,
desde las aguas turbias
que ya no son azules
pasos que nos alzan su voz,
más allá de la espuma.

Hombre y mujer,
sobre el océano,
entre los aires mismos
de la nada,
de su alma acostumbrada
al vaivén de los ríos,
a la carne sonora
de su ébano,
a la flácida luz
del monte umbrío
que los entorna
en su torno infinito.

Mujer y hombre
lado a lado,
del bosque a la montaña,
de la ceiba a la luna,
con lanzas en los labios,
con el ojo de buey
entre las manos,
con un manto elegíaco
para cada pupila,
con un árbol de paz,
entre los dos.

Black Couple

Ocean passages
and baobab yearnings,
from muddied waters
no longer blue,
passages shouting to us
beyond the foam.

Man and woman,
above the ocean,
among the very winds
of nothingness,
of their souls, accustomed
to the play of rivers,
to their ebony's
resonant flesh,
to the faint light
of the shadowy woodland
that surrounds them
in its infinite surroundings.

Woman and man
side to side
from forest to mountain,
from ceiba to moon,
with lances in their lips,
with the porthole
between their hands,
with an elegiac shade
for each pupil,
with a tree of peace
between them.

(D.F.)

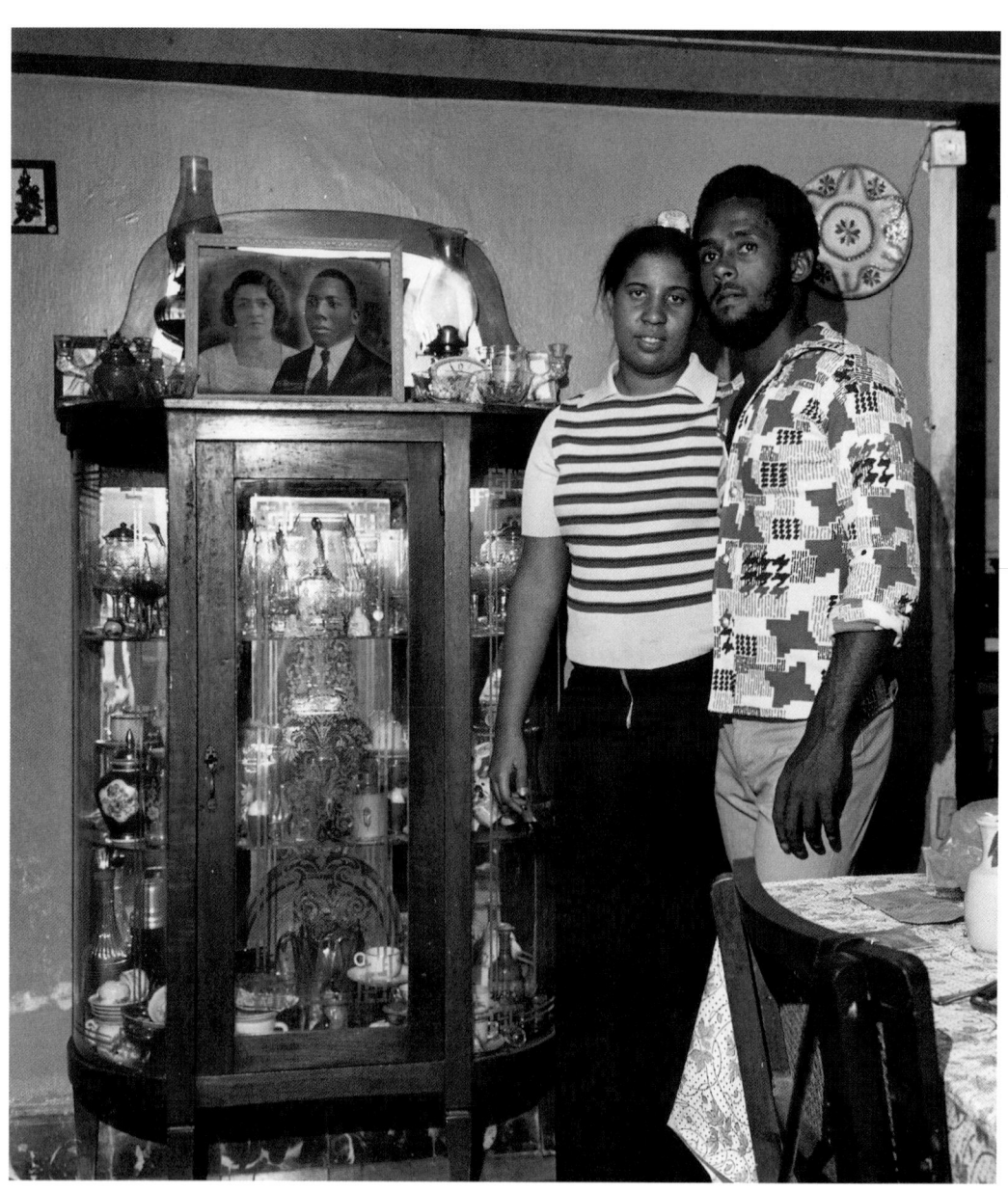

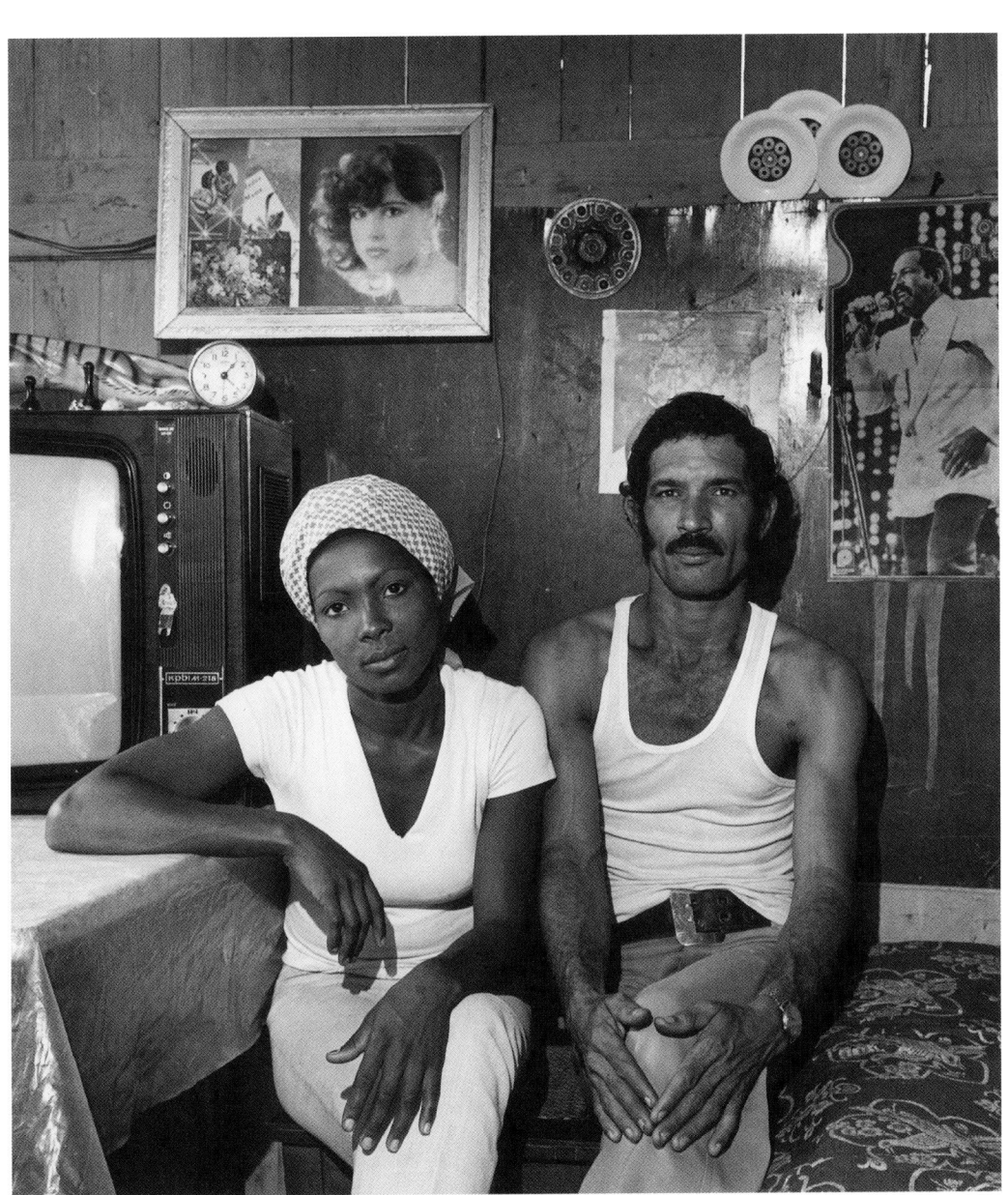

Instante

Ayer, ella no comprendió las matemáticas
pero leyó con gusto una historia de África
donde contaban cosas
de tráfico y galeones.
Hoy, él fundó una novena para jugar pelota
y donó sangre en el hospitalito provincial.
Ella corrió toda una pista
y él fue a comprar almejas deliciosas
en un mercado.
Él soñaba con indias lavando todas a la orilla del río.
Ella fue a la nevera
y, con un placer casi prohibido,
devoró las almejas que él había conseguido
en el mercado.
Son las cuatro y diez de la tarde.
Ambos están mirando el mismo lente
y han compartido la misma esperanza.

Instant

Yesterday, mathematics eluded her,
but she read with delight a history of Africa
where they recounted facts
about slave trade and galleons.
Today he rounded up nine guys to play baseball
and donated blood at the county clinic.
She ran around the entire track,
and he shopped for tasty mussels
at the market.
He dreamed about Indian girls, all washing at the riverbank.
She went to the refrigerator
and, with a nearly forbidden pleasure,
devoured the mussels he'd managed to buy
at the market.
It is four-ten in the afternoon.
Both gaze into the same lens
and share the same hope.

(P.C.)

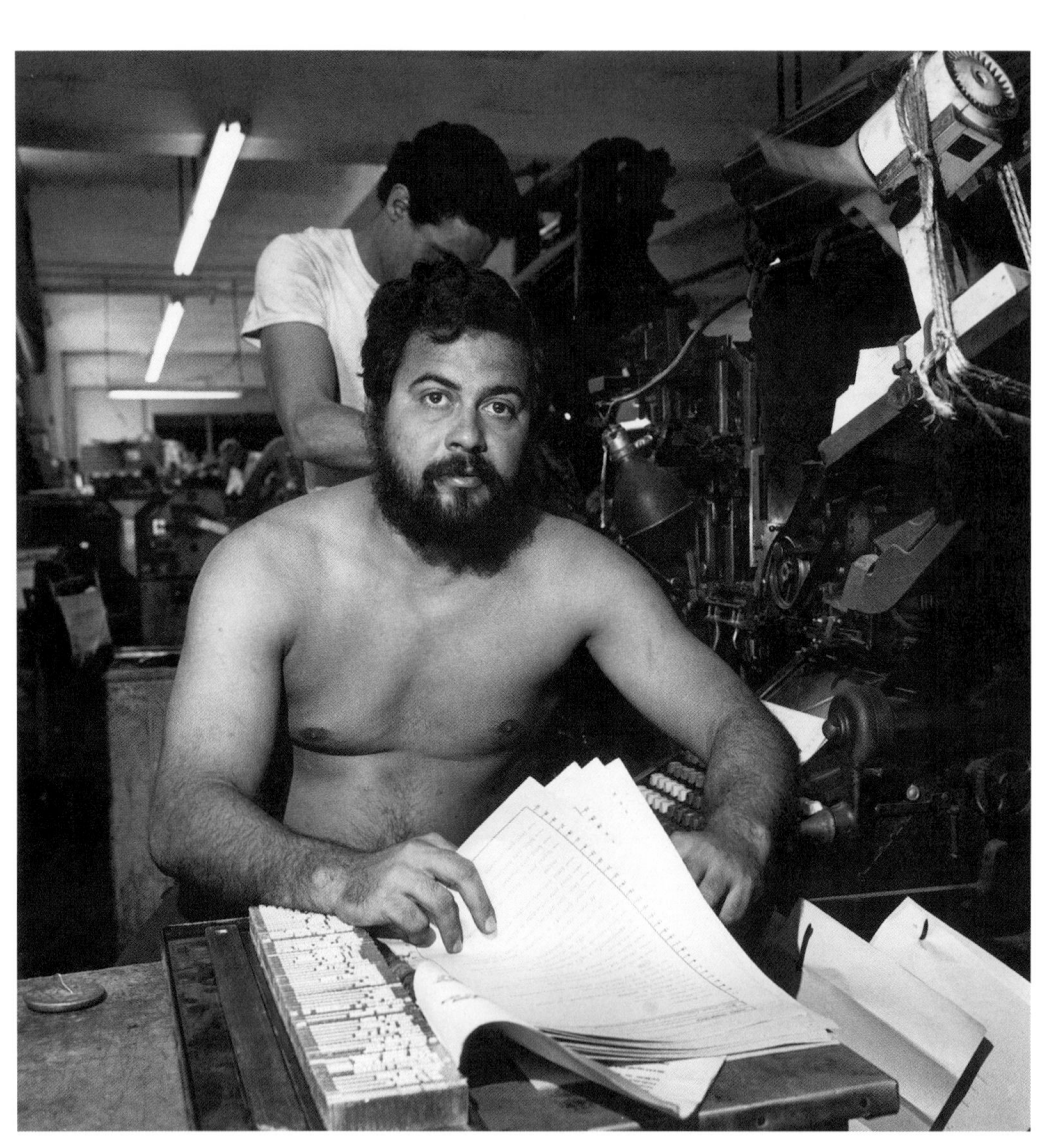

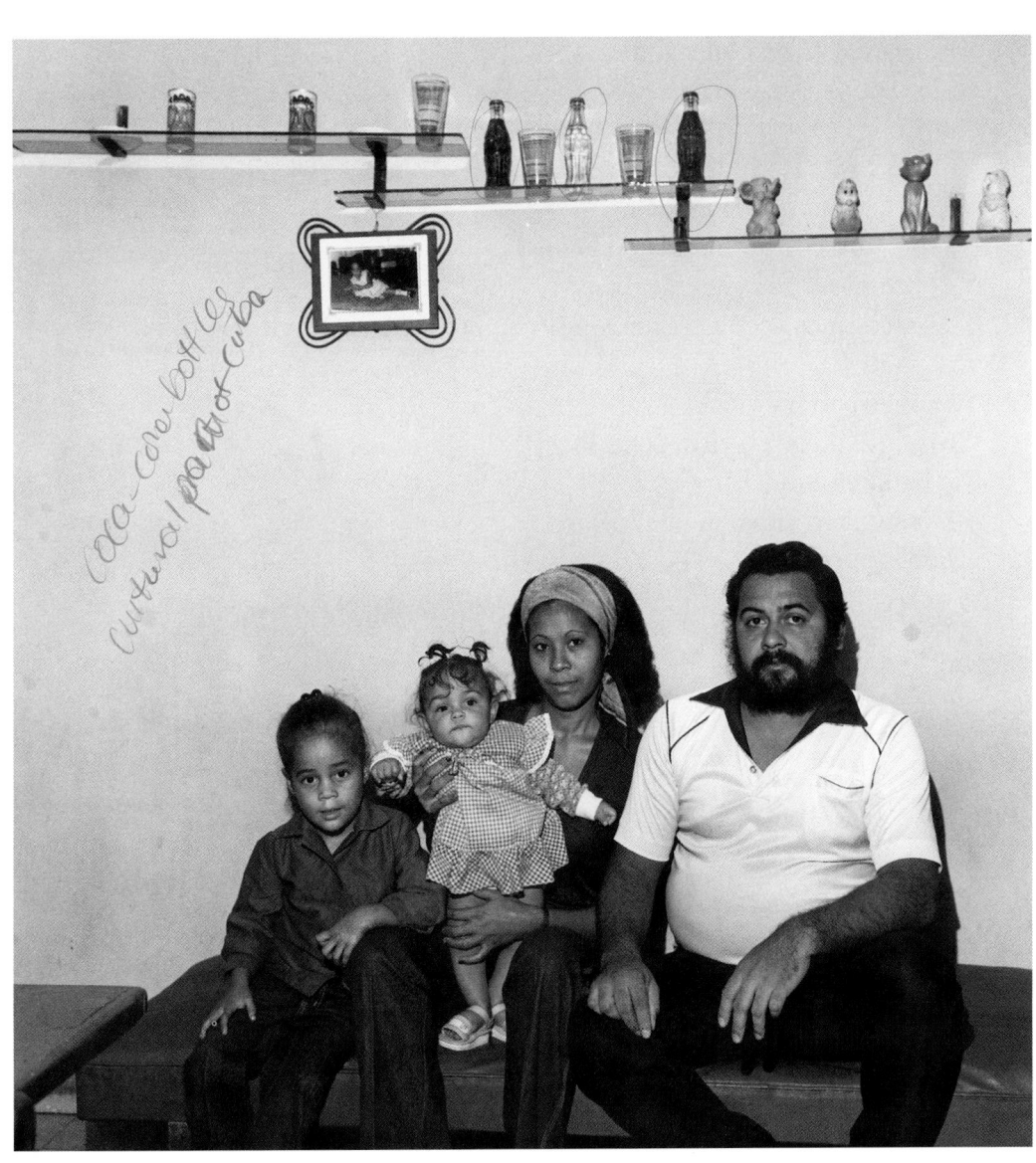

Hora de la verdad (IX)

Y canto en Cuba.
Canto en mi lengua para siempre.
Pasan los jóvenes con sus melenas rojas
cernidas por el viento de la Revolución,
con su proa al sol de nuestro Nuevo Mundo.
Y nado sobre la ciudad.
Y sobre el azul de la ciudad,
y sobre la vicisitud habida de la ciudad.
Y sobre su última generación.
Y construimos y construimos por encima del aislamiento
y de la usura.
Yo quiero estar aquí.
Cruzando puentes, ríos, centrífugas.
Me baño en níquel:
—Desentierro la lengua del pájaro.
Qué lindo mi país.

Hour of Truth (IX)

And I sing in Cuba.
Sing in my native tongue forever.
Young people pass by with their tufts of red hair
floating in the wind of Revolution,
its prow turned to the sun of our New World.
And I swim above the city.
And above the blue of the city,
and above the sudden change in the city.
And above its latest generation.
And we're building and building, higher than our isolation,
higher than their profiteering.
Here's where I want to be.
Crossing bridges, rivers, centrifuges.
I dip myself in nickel:
—I unearth the bird's tongue.
How lovely is my land.

[handwritten: Embracing Blackness or Cubanidad?]

(D.F.)

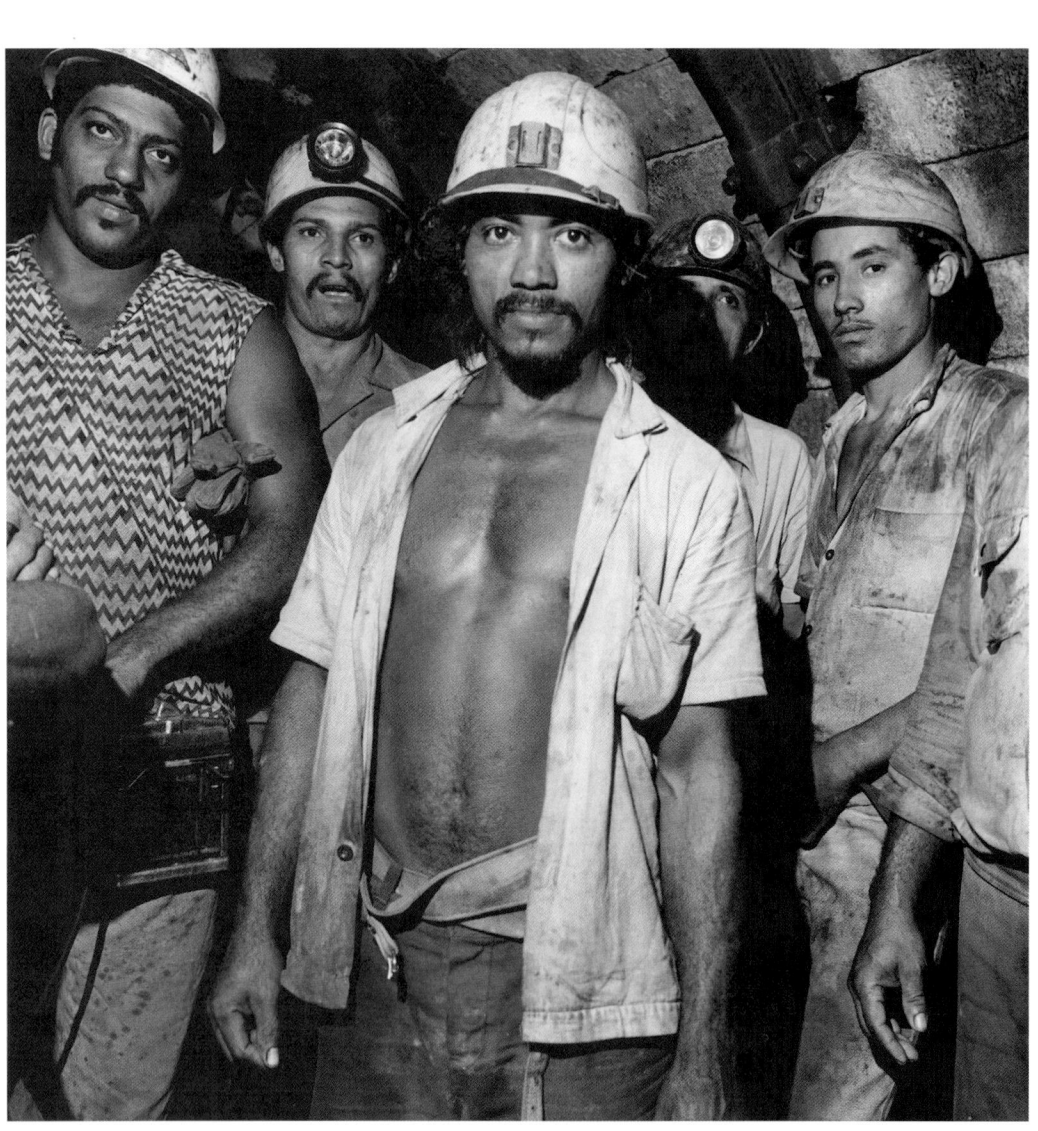

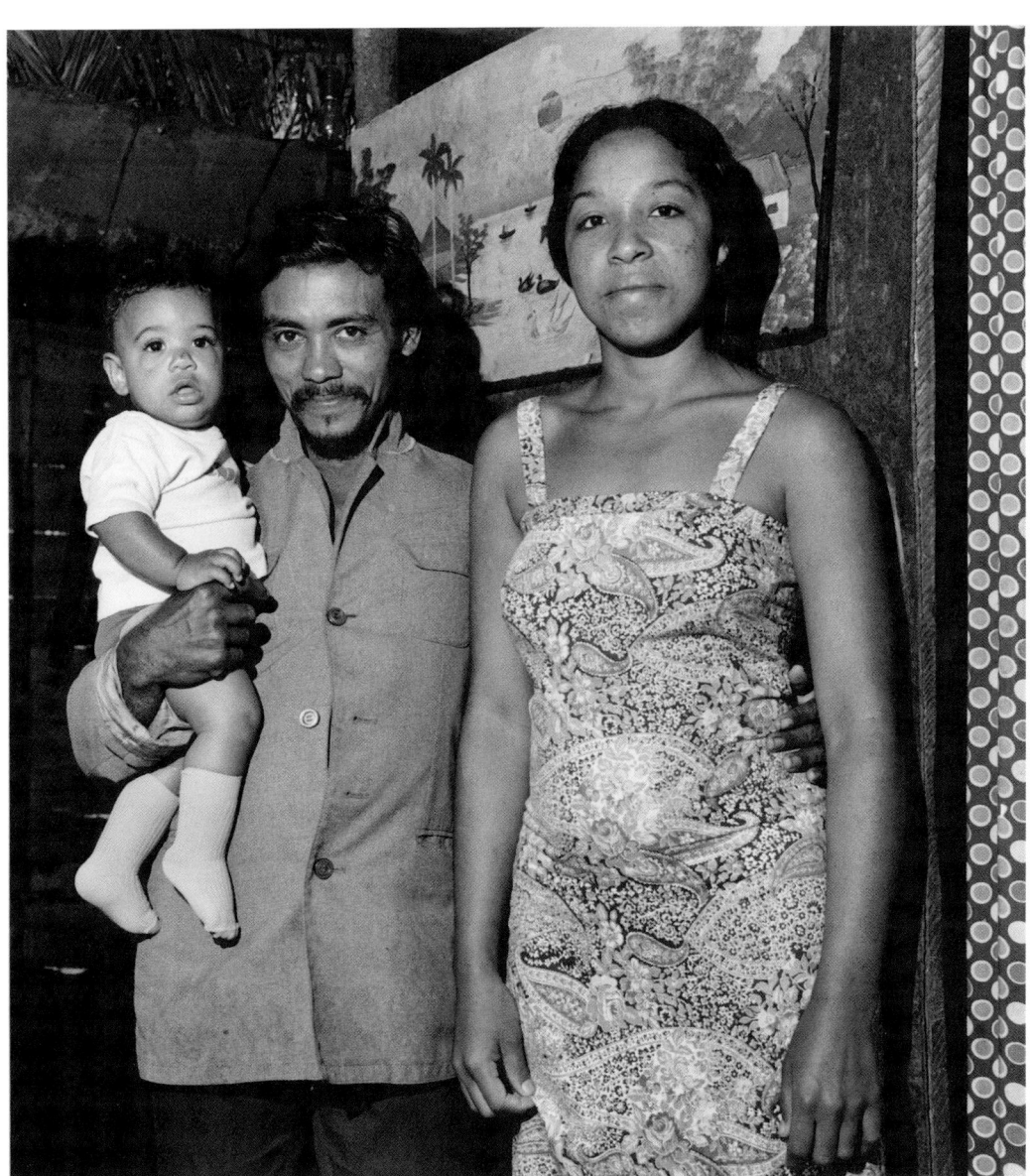

En Moa

> *Intentando escribir el último poema para los mineros de Moa*
> *que retrató el lente de mi amigo Milton Rogovin*

¿Qué luz esperan estos mineros,
estos rostros de los mineros
que sacan la luz de las entrañas
de un pueblo extraño y rojo y polvoriento
que, alguna vez, nombraron Moa?
Necesitamos esa luz
más que nunca
cuando se acaba este siglo
que transpira sangre,
y es casi una dama sofisticada
que pudo visitar las estrellas.

En Moa
también se está acabando el siglo
pero no el esplendor de la luz
esparcida en los ojos de los mineros,
del minero con una criatura en brazos
cuya existencia no conocerá
el fragor de las balas de la Sierra Cristal
pero sí el canto de los gallos
en la mañana.

Los mineros seguirán buscando esa luz oculta en la tierra de Moa.
Y detendrán la muerte.
Fueron estos mineros
los que escucharon mi triste canción.

In Moa

> *Trying to Write the Last Poem for the Miners of Moa*
> *Whose Portraits Were Taken by the Lens of My Friend Milton Rogovin*

What light can these miners hope for,
these faces of miners
who extricate light from the entrails
of a strange red dustbedeviled village
that someone once decided to call Moa?
We need this light
now more than ever
at the end of a century
that lives and breathes blood
and that almost became a sophisticated lady
who might have visited the stars.

In Moa
too, the century is ending,
but not the radiance of the light
glittering in the eyes of miners,
of the miner holding in his arms a babe
whose life will never know
the clamor of bullets in the Sierra Cristal,
but who instead will hear the crowing cock
at break of day.

The miners will still search for that light hidden in the land of Moa.
And they will stop death.
These were the very miners
who listened to the sadness of my song.

(D.F.)

Nancy Morejón

Born in the Los Sitios district of Central Havana on August 7, 1944, Nancy Morejón is the only child of tobacco worker and dressmaker Angélica Hernández and Felipe Morejón, who worked as a stevedore in the Havana docks. As a young man, her father worked as a merchant marine and spent long periods in the United States, where he came to know and love a vast jazz culture that he would later share with his daughter. Her mother's Chinese and European ancestry and the African ancestry of her father created a blended duality in the poet, who eventually embraced the notion of transculturation. Morejón believes there is no Spanish or African purity in the New World but rather a biological and cultural fusion that resulted in a different culture embracing both, though "profoundly marked by the terrible and prolonged episode of slavery," according to Juanamaría Cordones-Cook.

Just fourteen years old when the Cuban Revolution took place, Morejón benefitted from the opening of the doors of culture, education, and the arts to people who had previously been excluded, and she crowned her educational achievements with a magna cum laude degree in French Language and Literature from the University of Havana. She has translated numerous acclaimed French authors including Arthur Rimbaud, Paul Éluard, René Depestre, Édouard Glissant and Ernest Pépin, and her books of criticism of the work of Nicolás Guillén are considered classics.

Although not a member of the Communist Party, she realized how much her social circumstances had improved because of the Revolution and became an active participant in the intellectual life of her island. The Revolution became an essential part of her work. Always closely aligning herself with the have-nots, she, like Milton Rogovin, found inspiration in the humble and anonymous.

While many of her compatriots emigrated from Cuba, Morejón remained loyal to her roots. She did not, however, become alienated from those who left and, indeed, they became a personal preoccupation. These people, she believed, could never cut the roots that tied them to Cuba and would remain out of place in the world.

So, too, she could never cut her African roots. Until Morejón appeared, the Afro-Hispanic woman was unseen in literature. Marginalized by gender, race, and social class, Afro-Hispanic women were invisible and silenced. As revolution spread through the Caribbean, however, these women began to be heard, and it was Morejón who initiated and established a tradition of Afro-Hispanic poetry by women. She does not believe, however, that "women's narrative" exists, and she does not think of herself as a feminist; rather, she believes that literary and artistic creations reflect the human condition.

Morejón published her first book, *Mutismos,* in 1962. This was followed by twelve collections of her poems, three monographs, a play, and four volumes of critical studies of Cuban and Caribbean history and literature. Additionally, numerous poems and articles that she wrote have appeared in anthologies, literary journals, and in the mass media. She has collaborated with painters, sculptors, artisans, dancers, playwrights, actors, musicians, and singers, and has even attained fame as a lyricist. Her work has been translated into more than ten languages. Her fame crosses national, cultural, and ideological boundaries.

Morejón worked as director of the Caribbean Studies Center at the Casa de las Americas, epicenter of the Latin American literary community, for seven years before leaving to concentrate on her own writing. Morejón frequently visited the United States to lecture and teach at various cultural institutions and universities until changes in policy under President George W. Bush made travel from Cuba almost impossible. She returned to once again lead the Caribbean Studies Center in May of 2000. She was awarded the National Literary Award 2001 in Havana. A large selection of her work, *Looking Within/Mirar Adentro,* was published in a bilingual edition by Wayne State University Press, Detroit, Michigan, in 2003, as part of their African American Life Series.

Milton Rogovin

"The rich have their own photographers...I photograph the forgotten ones."

Milton Rogovin was born in New York City in 1909. He graduated from Columbia University in 1931 with a degree in optometry and after practicing in New York for several years, moved to Buffalo in 1938, where he established his own optometric practice. Nineteen forty-two was an auspicious year: he married Anne Snetsky—who would be his collaborator, organizer, and companion across five continents for fifty years—purchased his first camera, and was inducted into the U.S. army, where he served as an optometrist until 1945. Upon his discharge, he returned to his optometric practice and his growing family. By 1947, the Rogovins had two daughters, Ellen and Paula, and a son, Mark.

Rogovin was called before the House Committee on Un-American Activities in 1957; the *Buffalo News* headline about his testimony named him "Buffalo's Top Red." The persecution that followed significantly impacted his business, and in 1958, he picked up his camera and began to capture images that communicated his deep desire for a more just and equal society. He later stated that though his voice had been silenced, *he* would not be silenced.

His first photographic series, documenting storefront church services in Buffalo, took three years to complete, and in 1962, this work was published in *Aperture*, a prestigious photography publication in the United States. Introduced by noted African American historian W.E.B. DuBois, the article introduced Rogovin's work to an audience beyond Buffalo. That summer he and Anne traveled to Appalachia, where he photographed miners and their families. He returned and continued his work there each summer through the early 1980s. The 1960s saw numerous exhibits of his work at prestigious museums, as well as his first trip to Chile, at the invitation of Pablo Neruda, where he collaborated with the Nobel Prize-winning poet on a series of images and words.

In 1972, Rogovin received a Master of Arts in American Studies from the University at Buffalo, and he was appointed instructor of documentary photography at the institution, where he taught through 1974. That same year, he began to photograph Buffalo's Lower West Side, a project that eventually documented more than one hundred families. Milton and Anne Rogovin returned to the neighborhood in 1984, 1992, and 2002, providing tremendous insight into the lives of Puerto Rican, Mexican, African American, Native American and Italian families over thirty years.

In 1981 he returned to Appalachia to photograph women coal miners, and traveled to France to photograph miners there. The following year found him photographing miners in Scotland. He was awarded the coveted W. Eugene Smith Award for Documentary Photography in 1983, which allowed Anne and him to travel to China, Cuba, Czechoslovakia, France, Germany, Mexico, and Zimbabwe to continue his series on miners.

Throughout his accomplished career, Rogovin's work has appeared in more than 160 journals, magazines and other publications. He has participated in more than thirty group shows, sixty solo exhibitions all over the world, and has had eight books published on his photography. His photographs are in the permanent collections of over two dozen prominent museums, including the Biblotheque Nationale in Paris, the Museum of Modern Art in New York, the J. Paul Getty Museum in Los Angeles, and the Victoria and Albert Museum in London. In 1999, the Library of Congress acquired 1,200 of his photographs, all of his negatives, and contact sheets as part of the Library's collection. He was the first living photographer to be so recognized in thirty years.

Rogovin's lens illuminated prominent social issues of the day: the effect of the economic embargoes on the Cuban people, the plight of the miner in ten nations, the decline of the steel industry in Buffalo, the common struggle of the poor living in Buffalo's Lower West Side, the pride of the people of Chile, and the celebration of spirit in the storefront churches of Buffalo. Rogovin's sole purpose—as timeless as it is universal—is to help the viewer see the people in his photographs in a new light: as people of strength and dignity.

The Translators

Pamela Carmell teaches Spanish in St. Louis and is a founding member of the St. Louis Translators Roundtable. She has translated Luisa Valenzuela, Ena Lucía Portela, Mirta Yáñez, and Carlos Cortés, among others, and her translations have appeared in numerous magazines and anthologies. Her translation of Antonio Larreta's novel *The Last Portrait of the Duchess of Alba*, was a Book-of-the-Month Club selection. Her translation of poems by Belkis Cuza Malé, *Woman on the Front Lines*, received the Witter Bynner Prize.

David Frye teaches Latin American society and culture at the University of Michigan - Ann Arbor. He has translated a number of books, including *Thine Is the Kingdom* and *Distant Palaces* by Cuban novelist and poet Abilo Estévez (Arcade Publishing, 1999 and 2004) and *The Mangy Parrot* by José Joaquín Fernandez de Lizardi (Hackett Publishing, 2004), for which he was awarded a Translation Fellowship by the National Endowment for the Arts, and is the author of *Indians into Mexicans: History and Identity in a Mexican Town* (University of Texas Press, 1996).